Pre-release Acclaim fo

"Howard Adamsky's new book is both a passionate call to arms for a better world of work and a no-nonsense manual for the individual who is prepared to get (back) into it.

"In a situation where many have either lost their jobs or been forced to see their career opportunities diminish radically, Howard comes out swinging, and for once, a book on job-getting truly feels like it's on the side of the worker. *Employment Rage* can evoke many feelings—anger, passion, fighting spirit—but in the end it's a book about hope and possibility. Read it, get enraged, and get working!"

—Professor Alf Rehn,
Chair of Management and Organization
at Åbo Akademi University (Finland).www.alfrehn.com

....

"In the face of challenging economic times, Adamsky offers advice that is professional, practical, and personal. His insights offer hope for surviving and prospering in a new marketplace. A must read for all engaged in the world of work."

—Kenny Moore, Author
The CEO and the Monk:
One Company's Journey to Profit and Purpose.
http://www.kennythemonk.typepad.com

....

"With all of his classical candor and down to earth style of writing, Howard Adamsky has done it again with *Employment Rage*. Perhaps it should be subtitled: Reality Therapy for the Unemployed.

"Unlike many of the career guidance pundits who perpetually publish advice on the ideal way to deal with job loss, Howard has lived from both sides of the desk. When someone speaks out who personally recruited and hired thousands, and who also fell victim to the 'corporate axe', you know it's from well-tested experience. And while we've all heard of the classical 'stages of shock' one must go through when the unexpected happens, Howard brings theory down to a pragmatic and actionable level in a heart-felt and all too human manner, then offers solid advice and practical solutions.

"*Employment Rage* should be read by not just the unemployed, but by those who even today remain at work—in preparation for the changes that continue to wreak havoc on what we used to believe was 'the world of work.'"

—Dan Kilgore
A Recruiting Professional with over 35 years' experience
in the field, and a Principal Consultant with Riviera Advisors,
a global corporate employment process consulting firm.

Employment
RAGE

What You've Lost and How to Win it Back

Howard Adamsky

Printed in the United States of America

ISBN: 978-1-935254-46-1

Cover Design by NorLightsPress Graphic Department
Book Design by Nadene Carter

First printing, 2011

Dedication

To my brother Douglas, who still looks out for me. Many thanks.

To the memory of my father, my father-in-law, Judy and Shawn.

"Yes, to dance beneath the diamond sky with one hand waving free
Silhouetted by the sea, circled by the circus sands
With all memory and fate driven deep beneath the waves
Let me forget about today until tomorrow"
—*Bob Dylan*

I do not paint things. I only paint the difference between things.
—*Henri Matisse*

"Still, when I think of the
road we're traveling on
I wonder what's gone wrong
I can't help it, I wonder what's gone wrong"
—*Paul Simon*

Working Definitions

Employment is a contract between two parties, one being the employer and the other being the employee. An **employee** may be defined as: "A person in the service of another under any contract of hire, express or implied, oral or written, where the employer has the power or right to control and direct the employee in the material details of how the work is to be performed." Black's Law Dictionary page 471 (5th ed. 1979).

In a commercial setting, the employer conceives of a productive activity, generally with the intention of generating a profit, and the employee contributes labour to the enterprise, usually in return for payment of wages. Employment also exists in the public, non-profit and household sectors.

Source: Wikipedia

In psychiatry, **rage** is a mental state that is one extreme of the intensity spectrum of anger. When a person experiences rage it usually lasts until a threat is removed or the person under rage is incapacitated. The other end of the spectrum is annoyance (DiGiuseppe & Tafrate, 2006). Psycho-pathological problems such as depression increase the chances of experiencing feelings of rage (Painuly et al., 2005).

Source: Wikipedia

Employment Rage is the almost uncontrollable seething fury and frustration that arises in people who have been employed all of their lives and are simply unable to identify and secure the employment required to continue to lead meaningful lives due to circumstances that are often beyond their control.

Source: Howard Adamsky

Acknowledgement

So many people, events, and ideas make up the foundation of writing a book, and to these individuals I will always be grateful.

To my childhood friends Juicy Brucie, Honest John, Marty the K, Wayne, Freddie, Larry and all the Echo Mountain crew: heartfelt thanks for the memories and companionship we shared. To quote Tolkin, Elen sila lumenn' omentielvo "A star shines on the hour of our meeting" (by Frodo to Gildor)

To John Amodeo, a dear friend and advisor on this book: your help was instrumental in every aspect of shaping, editing, and guiding me on the original manuscript. For your advice and council, I will be forever grateful.

To my friend Steve Levy who is always there to answer my questions. www.recruitinginferno.com and @levyrecruits on Twitter.

To Anthony Bordain who showed me one *can* write with anger and passion. http://blog.travelchannel.com/anthony-bourdain and @noreservations on Twitter.

To my dear friend Alf Rehn: I thank you for putting up with my manic and daily emails for over a month, telling you how many words I wrote each day. A lesser friend would have killed me. www.alfrehn.com and @alfrehn on Twitter.

To my family, of whom I am very proud: Bill and Jake and Nick. I hope all of you go on to be happy and do great things. Also, do not ask for money because I won't get rich from this book.

To the folks at ERE Media: my thanks for your commitment to create a great place for recruiters to visit, share, and learn.

To my friend Bill Berens who read the manuscript in hardcopy and made wonderful and enlightening comments on almost every page. I thank you so much.

Lastly to my wife, who inspires me with her courage every single day.

Contents

A Word to the Wise *1*

Introduction *3*

Chapter 1: *I Know How You Feel.* *9*

Chapter 2: *You Are Not Guilty* *13*

Chapter 3: *Assigning Blame is a Fool's Delight* *19*

Chapter 4: *Atrocities for Your Consideration* *23*

Chapter 5: *The Underbelly of Corporate America* *31*

Chapter 6: *Active and Passive Candidates*
Lord Help the Unemployed *41*

Chapter 7: *Ask Not What Networking Can Do For You* *45*

Chapter 8: *Headhunters: A Crash Course.* *57*

Chapter 9: *You're Working on Your Resume—Again?.* *65*

Chapter 10: *Got References?* *75*

Chapter 11: *The Interview: Insights and Essential Thinking.* . . *83*

Chapter 12: *Go with Your Strengths* *97*

Chapter 13: *Innovate for Professional Survival* *103*

Chapter 14: *Who's Managing YOUR Career?* *107*

Chapter 15: *Animal House is Extinct.* *111*

Chapter 16: *The Recent Graduate.* *115*

Chapter 17: *Gornish* *123*

Chapter 18: *My Story.* *135*

Chapter 19: *Social Media, Employment, and You.* *141*

Chapter 20: *Great Expectations: A Chapter for Recruiters* *155*

Chapter 21: *What To Do Now* *163*

Chapter 22: *Closing Thoughts* *187*

About the Author *189*

End Notes *189*

A Word to the Wise

"You can have anything in life you want, but you can't have everything in life you want."
—Kevin's father

Success is a Push Business

On some days I can hardly drag myself out of bed. I'm tired or it's raining—perhaps both. Some days my mind doesn't want to engage, and I have no energy for the good fight. I imagine getting in my car and returning to Brooklyn, where I'll slowly walk Franklin Avenue from President Street to Park Place and remember a life that was far less complex—far less dangerous. On those days, I find it more appealing to just sit and think than push the ball another few inches up the hill.

I suspect you have these days as well. I believe all of the above issues are good reasons to give ourselves a reprieve—take the day off and get lost in our wide screen television or continue reading to see if Lisbeth and Blomkvist wind up together in the end. But I don't do this, and I suggest you don't do it either.

The thin line between success and failure often rests upon our ability to push. Our brilliance, resources, support from others, or magnificent plans won't make the difference; it depends upon our ability to press on through the pain, exhaustion, and frustration of life's roadblocks. Unfortunately, exhaustion is not a good enough reason to take the day off.

Look around you. The light bulb, the airplane, and the book you're reading. All this took hard, focused effort. Behind everything we take for granted is a hero—a person who didn't rest for the rain, the moon, the stars, or the tears.

Great things often happen through the driving force of one person who finds more reasons to press on than to rest— even when that rest is well deserved.

I try to live this way and succeed much of the time, but certainly not every day.

I hope you can try hard as well. I hope you find the strength to persevere through all the pain, disappointment, and the distress of everything that doesn't happen for you. I hope you can live through the unfairness of it all and continue with your mission. If you do, I can't guarantee the universe will relent and give you what you seek. On the other hand, I can promise you a far greater chance of being successful if you continue to push on and persist in that effort every single day.

Introduction

"Come, my friends,
'Tis not too late to seek a newer world."
—Lord Alfred Tennyson

My Mission and Purpose

*A*s a rule, I dislike self-help books. To me, they usually offer a hope for change combined with a seductive sense of ease—an overly simple route to solving complex, multifaceted problems. I warn you now, this is not a typical self-help book. I believe the last thing the world needs is another book that tells you how to get a job, fix your career, or become the slim person who lives within you.

This book is a manuscript of concepts and ideas—a book filled with observations and new realities. It's a book that looks at what has happened to you professionally, the effect it's had on you, and real world opportunities for change and progress. We'll consider the different and converging angles you can take as you move from survival to success.

I wrote *Employment Rage* from start to finish in 23 days. I mention this because writing a full manuscript in 23 days means you have a lot on your mind—content you strongly believe in and fingers that burn up the keyboard. It also means you have a passion for what you're doing.

Here's how to best use the four parts of this book:

The first section explores the pain we all feel since the economy collapsed. It deals with the frustration, anger, and helplessness so many of us live with every day. I hope you'll see it as a reality check on all we've suffered and what we continue to endure.

The second part is advice and counsel: insights from an expert who deals with employment all day long. Here, you'll gain perspective and opinions on how to identify and secure new opportunities. It even includes a chapter for people who are going off to college, those who just graduated, and those who are fortunate enough to be employed.

The third part is short and to the point—an overview of my life since the meltdown. Through reading this, I hope you'll come to understand me as I believe I understand you.

The fourth part of the manuscript is future-oriented, dealing with what we must do as individuals to prepare ourselves and be successful in a world that has the potential to give us much, but will ask for much in return. This section deals with far more than what we must do. It outlines what we must become. It speaks to how we must evolve and shake off the ennui that robs us of our agility, imagination, and capacity to fly. I see it this way: the same old things will yield the same old you. The execution of the new and the different will create a shiny new you. Can you imagine the possibilities?

Micro to macro in scope, *Employment Rage* is deeply personal because it talks about you and about me. From the heart to the wallet, this book gives you an enhanced vantage point from which to consider and ultimately pursue your professional goals and regain a semblance of what you've lost: self-respect, ego, employment, and a sense of purpose.

This book is designed to help you understand, on a host of different levels, what happened to you and your career. It's all here: the rage and helplessness, coupled with a deep sense of loss and pain over the meltdown of our economy.

Employment Rage deals with more than the economy's effect on your daily life, including how it touches your family, your sense of worth, and all of the things you consider important. I wrote this book as an industry insider who wants to speak directly and honestly with you. I want to connect with as many people as I can, and therein lays the real value of my contribution.

Other authors could have written slices of this book, but it took an employment insider to write it all. It also took a fellow victim of this economy. My objective is to speak of my own personal pain right along with yours, because I do understand.

Tricks and tips? Sure, endless things contained within the pages will be of great value. For example, do you think you know all about headhunters? I'll bet there's much you can learn in that chapter, which contains ideas and commentary for working with these largely misunderstood employment professionals.

Have you worked on your resume again today? How about yesterday? Perhaps tomorrow? If so, you might be doing the "I'm working on my resume dance." The resume chapter will certainly help you stop obsessing.

Do you approach networking because you need help? That's the wrong orientation. How about the interview? Think you have that down cold? Look at the insights offered and you may reconsider your position. Do you believe you're perfect for a specific job, and you'll ace the interview? If so, you'll have much to think about as you read the chapter on interviewing, because it doesn't work that way.

How is Toastmaster's going? Not an active member? I strongly suggest you read that chapter first and join a local group. Toastmasters may be the best move you can ever make for your career and professional life. Read the chapter and find out why.

Do you understand the fundamental concepts of Social Networking and how it relates to your career aspirations? Do you understand how it can supercharge your results and make things happen? If not, the chapter entitled "Social Media, Employment, and You" will open both your eyes as well as your mind.

Do you believe life inside corporate America is for you? Perhaps you're right, but first read the chapter entitled "The Ugly Underbelly of Corporate America" and tell me if I've been there or not. Just be sure to hold your nose, because it's an ugly business; a slaughterhouse with wing tips.

This is not a book of pedagogy. It's a book of ideas designed for people who are sick and tired of it all, but have little idea how to make a better life for themselves.

It's a book for those who want to know more about employment from the person who actually reads your resume; the person who confers with hiring managers on tactical decisions every day—a guy who's a headhunter, a public speaker, and an author. From a person who attempts to look at his world of work with creativity and insight in order to create real value; a man who stubbornly refuses to repackage the old, tired ideas that worked when Clinton was president; a man who offers solutions to the entrenched problems we face in 2011.

I hope you'll consider this book a tool for navigating the new world of work in this dysfunctional and stagnant economy. To use it in a way that will allow you to reflect upon and examine all that happened to your career and your life. To then take action to use that insight and information to redirect your efforts to sculpt a better and more satisfying existence. Part manifesto, part tell-all, and part road map for success, *Employment Rage* will put new possibilities into your hands and illuminate things you didn't see—or worse, saw incorrectly. Self-help book? Lets just say it will help you big time.

This book is the best thing going if you work it to your advantage. Will you agree with every single line? Perhaps not, because thinkers seldom do. I hope we can partner on this and create a better outcome for you and all of the people in your life.

Robert Frost said, "Very often, the only way out, is through." Let's get through this together, and then do what we can to get the hell out.

Howard Adamsky
Stow, MA
1-18-11

Chapter 1

I Know How You Feel

For many people a job is more than an income; it's an important part of who we are. So a career transition of any sort is one of the most unsettling experiences you can face in your life.

—Paul Clitheroe

I Know What Your Day Is Like

*F*or a person who's unemployed, a typical day can be dismal. You awaken to a stark and jarring reality. You are unemployed and you must find a job. Soon. Money is tight, and hope is in short supply as well. With that realization, your first impulse it to turn over, shove your head under the pillow, and go back to sleep. Summoning the mental fortitude and willpower for job hunting is a huge challenge.

You procrastinate until you can no longer stand lying bed. You finally rise and head for the computer to check e-mail. Do you want Viagra or other pharmaceuticals? No problem. Need cheap fares on airlines and hotels, Facebook comments, or an occasional LinkedIn request? No problem. Looking for a special deal on a mortgage? It's all there. Everything's there except what you really need—an email from someone who's responding to your job search. That, my friend, is what you really need to see.

How about an answer on where things stand from that interview you had five weeks ago? Eight weeks ago? Three months ago? Sadly, no emails addressing any of that.

Welcome to the new normal, because that e-mail won't be arriving. You wonder what happened to the resumes you've sent. Have they been considered? Did a real person ever read them? Are they in a resume tracking system to be pulled up by a keyword search sometime in the next few months? Does anyone ever review them? Do they read your work history and compare your qualifications to the position for which you applied? How does resume submission work in today's job market?

You'd like to call human resources and get yourself noticed, but you can't get the name of a hiring manager. No one answers the phones and when you leave a message, they never return your call. Let me say that again for dramatic effect: Never. Most HRs check their messages at the beginning of the day and again at the end of day. They delete many calls without hearing the messages and usually don't give the callers a second thought.

They don't do this because they're bad people. Most folks in HR try hard to do what's right, but they're forced to deal with endless hordes of job hunters. The sheer number of people looking to them for help is overwhelming. Please keep in mind that in most organizations, human resources departments have been downsized to the bone; sliced and diced and killed by layoffs and attrition. If the HR folks spent even a few moments on the phone with everyone who wanted to talk about a position or the status of a resume, they would never have time to do anything else.

Now, back to your day.

You look at the clock and it's 11:38. Lunch is almost at hand, and you still haven't showered. You decide to clean up, go out for a bite of lunch, get some coffee, and shake off the angst. You put on a smile and decide to hit it hard when you return. Sitting over a sandwich, you realize the mail has probably arrived by now, which means more bills. You mentally go over the money you owe; what can be floated and what can't wait. Quarterly taxes? Condo fees? Your relationship with money is almost obsessive now, because you're tired of being broke. You're weary of figuring every angle until that next check arrives. Perhaps you'll make some calls to buy time and avoid opening the mail.

You notice people in the fast food place who are on their lunch break, wolfing down food so they can return to the job. You feel the familiar stab of loneliness you've come to think of as Job Envy.

This can't go on. Relief has to come sooner or later. A dinner out crosses your mind: a lovely thought. A glass of wine and quiet conversation would feel so civilized. But you're broke now, and the money would be better spent elsewhere

> You take another bite of your sandwich, feeling powerless in a world that changed overnight—a world where you don't have a safety net or an owner's manual for survival.

Lunch is done and it's 1:27. Time to face the computer again. You get home and check for the blinking light on your phone that would indicate a message.

Nothing.

You tell yourself that's no problem, because you're about to hit the job boards and this could be your big day. Away you go: Monster, Careerbuilder, Craigslist, and other niche sites you've come to know. You read the requirements, fill in endless fields to apply for a job, and hit the submit button. You experience a small sense of accomplishment with each submission; a hollow and fleeting kind of hope; an ephemeral sense of possibility and opportunity. You know in your heart that few things offer more hope, yet less chance for success, than submitting a resume online. But you do it anyway, because the alternative of doing nothing is even worse.

By 3:45 you aren't sure what to do next. You check LinkedIn

for positions, look for connections, and then dial a few friends you've spoken with over the years. You leave voice mails and move on. You go directly to the websites of organizations you admire or think might be hiring. You apply for more positions. The quiet is deafening and you feel alone. By 4:45 your brain hurts, your mouth is dry, and your neck and shoulders are knotted with tension. You check e-mail again. Nothing important. You close up shop and the day is done. Now you can transition into the early evening.

What to do tonight? Should you go to a local Better Business Bureau or similar networking event so you can be with other people like yourself? Does misery love company that much? Do you want to spend two hours listening to people give well-rehearsed elevator speeches designed to sound natural and off the cuff, as they then say; "…and what do you do?"

You try to relax, but life without work just doesn't feel right. The fact that you aren't working is always on your mind.

You depend on no one and no one depends on you. For most of us, work gives our lives meaning: a stake in the earth; a place in society where we feel grounded. You need to work. You want to work. You have talent, ability, and experience—yet no one will hire you. You think about changing careers. Could you become a chef, a social worker, a teacher, or a writer? Could you become a carpenter? Open a bed and breakfast? Would life be better if you moved to the city? To the country? To a totally different country? How on earth can you fix this problem?

You watch television, read a bit, and perhaps spend time with your family. At 11 p.m. you fall asleep and awaken the next day to the same reality. This is not a fun time in your life. Let's keep going and see how you can fix this cycle of pain and frustration.

Chapter 2
You Are Not Guilty

*A great revolution is never the fault of the people
but the fault of the government.*

—Johann Wolfgang von Goethe

I find it interesting that when times are hard in some people's lives, the first thing they do is blame themselves. I know this is true, because I'm one of those people. Only after many years have I learned to recognize when a situation isn't my fault.

More than likely, if you're looking for work, you did nothing to deserve this. Through horrific luck, the collective forces of confluence, the crash of world markets, and astounding corporate malfeasance, we are enduring a perfect storm. Hellish and deep... with no end in sight.

Why did it all happen? The answer depends on whom you ask and their orientation. Those in the know point to the concept of expanding markets that created a bubble. They also speak to the forces that exist when a bubble can no longer be supported by the economic conditions upon which it was built. This, to a degree, is capitalism at work. Sadly, if we expect to live with the good side of capitalism, we also have to endure the bad. We have little choice, because to expect anything else is, well, not capitalism.

You need to focus on one simple fact: where the blame lies doesn't matter anymore. We're long past that point. The objective now? Move on and look ahead, because blame won't pay the bills.

We can learn a few lessons here. Might you have overspent on your mortgage? Bought stuff you didn't need? Did you replace prudent thinking with expensive wines, using a sense of false optimism as a plan of action? Was that your go-to-market scheme? Was "Let's just hope for the best" your new mantra? Perhaps you and I do share a splinter of culpability because we're human, and we all make mistakes. But surely the punishment does not fit the crime.

The point to remember is, in the scheme of things, when all of the jobs went away, many of us were left feeling bad about ourselves. If you're in that category, the time to stop is now. If you've been looking for a job for two years and still can't land one, that doesn't mean you're a failure, a has-been, or you lack marketable skills. The problem is, at the moment the need for your talent is limited by the supply and demand system, a hallmark of capitalism. We must all persevere until we reach solid footing once again.

I recently met with a senior sales executive I'll call Maria—a stellar person who, in better times, would have ten job offers, and people standing in line to hire her. She shared a bit of her story, which began with a sudden, unexpected layoff. She rebounded, quickly, landing a new job with a firm that was impressed by her ability to develop new business while maintaining relationships with existing customers. She's a one-person selling machine—smooth, but not slick, with a strong work ethic. Yet, she struggled in her new position as the economy melted down around her.

Even for those with an optimistic mindset, we know that (to quote Ron Jenkins back in 1963), "Something is wrong here; something is terribly wrong."* Every month we hear about bailouts,

---

* In describing the first moments of JFK's assassination, Dallas radio reporter Ron Jenkins said, "We cannot see who has been hit if anybody's hit, but apparently something is wrong here. Something is terribly wrong."

plunging markets, rising unemployment, and rampant mortgage foreclosures. A sense of doom hangs in the air—an economic hurricane Katrina. On an individual level, there's little one can do other than watch, wait, and wonder what effect it will have on you and your family. You *stand quietly at the shore* and brace yourself against the incoming tempest, hoping the tsunami will spare you. Nothing personal, but you hope it claims the other guy.

My sales friend Maria endured yet another layoff and watched her career evaporate. She found a new company, but their funding dried up and they closed their doors. She's again searching for work, but even getting interviews in this climate is an epic struggle. You want a job? You're lucky to get a phone screen. What now? She has custody of two children, ages three and seven. Her husband is gone, and he's also unemployed, with no money for child support. Her car is held together by bubblegum and duct tape, and the condo she calls home is sliding into foreclosure. Maria has endured six months of chaos as she struggles to develop a plan with the bank to stay put until things get better. *Until things normalize.* Until something happens.

I was fascinated by Maria's pilgrimage. Through all the misery, uncertainty, and fear, she told me that by far the single most dismal part of her plight was claiming her unemployment each week. Her lowest point wasn't about needing money; it wasn't about being in foreclosure; nor was it about struggling to live from week to week. The most depressing and miserable part of her new existence was the time she took every Monday to file that weekly unemployment claim. She told me she'd worked and supported herself all of her life, and at almost forty, having to ask the government for help made her feel helpless and miserable. The term she used was "wretched."

I do understand Maria's misery, and I know this woman desperately wants to work. She doesn't even want to collect unemployment while she spends time looking for her next job. Nearly all the people I know who are out of work or grossly underemployed truly *want* to work. They have talent, drive, and passion. They have all the knowledge, skills, and abilities that propelled them to success in the past. As I sit here writing, I consider my friends and business associates. I honestly can't think of a single person who wants to sit home and collect money from the state, burn through savings, or eat up retirement funds.

This is not the America I know, and it's frightfully far from the American dream to which so many of us aspire.

Perhaps I hang with an ambitious crowd, but most people I know are obsessed with going back to work and putting this nightmare behind them. I believe most of us who continue to push hard will come out the other end a bit bruised, but intact and successful. Unfortunately, we don't know when the end will come. To those who are suffering, I can only repeat that this situation isn't your fault, and I sincerely hope you don't blame yourself for the devastation we're all attempting to survive.

Why did I mention Maria's story? You may not be impressed by her plight because your own story could be far worse. At least she still has her condo and some cash coming in. You may have lost yours. Perhaps you and your spouse don't talk all that much anymore because this pain is almost too much to bear. You both quietly pick up scratch tickets and hope against hope that something will happen to rock your world. You aren't looking for riches; all you want in life, to quote Natalie Wood, is "yesterday." This longing doesn't seem unreasonable, because tomorrow seems awfully scary at the moment.

I tell Maria's story because she touched my life, and I want you to know I understand your situation. *I feel connected with you and I want to help.*

With deep despair and anger, I read Barbara Ehrenreich's seminal book entitled *Bait and Switch The (Futile) Pursuit of the American*

Dream.[1] This is the single most accurate description of what's happening to working people in this country. The author follows real people, like you and me, as they struggle to become reemployed. She shows how the rules of the employment game have drastically changed; our system of effort and reward has become broken, corrupt, and often devoid of the essential humanity we expect to find. We can live, to a degree, without prospects, money, jobs, and cars. We can live without many other things we once considered entitlements. What we cannot live without is *hope.* Living without hope is too much to bear.

Writer and speaker Les Brown speaks of misfortune in his life and always offers the same challenge: "It does not matter what happens to you. All that matters is, what are you going to do about it?"

I like this view of life, from a man who's had his share of misery and grief. Les also tells us, "Accept responsibility for your life. Know that it is you who will get you where you want to go, no one else." For him, loss of hope is not an option. He chooses hope.

I also choose hope, and that is my wish for you as well. I want you to continue this struggle with a sense of optimism and a belief that good things will happen.

> I want you to continue this struggle with a sense of optimism and a belief that good things will happen.

The bottom line: most of the time you can't control what happens to you. But you can learn to handle any situation with dignity, a bit of planning, and a lot of hope, despite difficult circumstances.

Chapter 3
Assigning Blame is a Fool's Delight

> *"Blame is just a lazy person's way*
> *of making sense of chaos."*
> —Doug Couplad

Studying the media in an attempt to understand our current state of affairs can be an angry business. Even a cursory observation demonstrates that blame is the biggest game in town. We view it on television and read it in print. Internet forums smolder with anger. Twitter runs endlessly with every possible opinion, while the blogosphere is on fire with unending accusations. Finger pointing and stories of culpability and governmental incompetence abound. The blame game will only intensify as things become more difficult from a financial perspective. As the saying goes, "You ain't seen nothin' yet." All rage; all day long. Good to have information? Of course, but not when it distracts you from your goals.

This blame can be sliced and diced into many categories, so let's simplify it into a couple of distinct groups. The first category is historical blame. We seek out those who caused our hurt and misery, our anger and fear. We point fingers, cite statistics, and hurl grenades in an attempt to respond and be heard. We want to stand up and be counted—and woe to those who disagree with us.

Was it Bush doctrine or the secret Skull and Bones crew? Was it the "vast right wing conspiracy" as alluded to by Hillary Clinton, or was it Obama and his secret pact with Israel that made us suffer? Was it Wall Street, or the mortgage guys? Was it the furniture makers and the skinheads who meet secretly in a bowling alley near Shobine every second Thursday who caused this catastrophe? Was it your boss? Tell me, who do you wish to blame? The responsibility for our misery must be assigned to someone.

The second category of blame relates to the future. This more dynamic category deals with what our government is allegedly doing, or not doing, to make our lives better or worse. This second category is endless, because instead of looking back to assign blame, we look forward to assign possibilities. This, my friends, is dicey stuff. This second category of blame is nonstop and maddening. The internal dialogue is often hateful, based upon your orientation and political viewpoint. We seek to uncover relevant facts, but please be advised that "facts" aren't as hard-edged as you might think. Facts are almost always in flux. Facts can look different, depending upon your vantage point.

Folks, for all our sakes, let's end the blame game now—right this minute. What's done is done. Putting aside both personal politics and blame, I believe we need to shape an America that will work for everyone—a centrist America. If we truly want to stop the blaming and build a great country, we need to arrive at a point of moderation, with the realization that no one will get everything they want, because the needs, rights, and responsibilities of our population are vast and contradictory. Anything our administration undertakes will appear to hurt one constituency and help another. I suspect that we will, for endless reasons, never move to an Atlas Shrugged world where John Galt holds court and laissez-faire capitalism, coupled with limited government, rules the day. We will always have some degree of collectivism and social agenda. On the other hand, we are a capitalist society. As such, we must bear the slings and arrows of our misfortune as well as our riches and our inequity, because capitalism guarantees neither stability nor fairness.

The purpose of my comments on the blame game is simple and direct. Do not waste any of your valuable time playing it. It may seem interesting and seductive, but blame will become a major distraction that slows you down.

I urge you to forget the blame game and get on with life. As a country, we have no choice but to do this. An America with so many people out of work is an America that is no longer working.

Playing the blame game will leave you bitter instead of better. Endless reading and postings to online forums won't get you where you want to go. Complaining that Obama is a socialist or every problem on the planet is the fault of Bush won't bring you any closer to making the car payment or figuring out how to float the mortgage a few extra days. Sadly, these dollar and cents problems demand vigilant attention, and addressing your employment situation should be number one on your mind.

Chapter 4

Atrocities for Your Consideration

> *"Indeed, history is nothing more than a tableau*
> *of crimes and misfortunes."*
> —Voltaire

*F*rom an economic and employment standpoint, our country is in a difficult place, and the last two years have been hell. As reported in August, 2010 by CNBC, "New U.S. claims for unemployment benefits unexpectedly climbed to a nine-month high last week, yet another setback to the frail economic recovery. Initial claims for state unemployment benefits increased 12,000 to a seasonally adjusted 500,000 in the week ending August 14, the highest since mid-November, the Labor Department said on Thursday. Analysts polled by Reuters had forecast claims slipping to 476,000 from the previously reported 484,000 the prior week, which was revised up to 488,000 in Thursday's report."

This is not good news.

I could easily fill page after page with studies and statistics, but in the end it doesn't matter how many people are unemployed. All that matters is your personal situation. If you, after endless struggles, reading self-help books, networking, and submitted resumes, still can't land a suitable job—that's the real problem. Nevertheless, let's take a moment to look at what has happened to our country and where we stand today.

For openers, we are in the most brutal and protracted recession since the bottom dropped out of the stock market in 1929. We've lost jobs in such staggering numbers that it's hard to even comprehend. But let's give it a try. If you see the recession starting in roughly January of 2008, as most economists seem to agree, as a country we've lost over eight million more jobs than we gained. Add this to lower tax revenues and increased bankruptcies, both personal and business, then stir mortgage defaults into the mix, and you have a recipe for catastrophe. This problem is directly linked to job loss, which creates a Catch 22 situation. When people are cautious with their money, consumer spending tightens. The demand for goods and services is greatly reduced and jobs disappear. People who've lost their jobs stop spending money, which further reduces the need for goods and services. And so it goes…

The following scenarios highlight what has happened over the past two years.

Stores and businesses we've known all our lives are closing their doors. Near my home, a store selling high end leather cases managed to hang on during all of the economic ups and downs of the last thirty years, including the dot-com bust, but this latest crisis sank them. Other small businesses in the area have also gone under. Multiply this by thousands of towns across the country and you can see the devastation to our small businesses. Consider the sheer number of jobs that vanished, the vendors affected, and the psychological effect of seeing your favorite place closed—looking like a dead body on display, with the windows waxed to keep out the curious.

Businesses that were too big to fail have declared bankruptcy. Examples include Washington Mutual, Lehman Brothers, and Worldcom, to name a few. These organizations hemorrhaged employees as tens of thousands of jobs disappeared. We've seen people being led out the front door by security guards, each employee clutching a box of personal belongings. It was ugly and humiliating. This was an American nightmare and the start of a new kind of a war. Each job lost represented a person who supported a family, had car payments, living expenses, and possibly a mortgage. Video clips showed displaced workers frozen in place along the curbside. Some embraced, while others sobbed. Those with microphones thrust in their faces said they had no clue about where to go, what to do, or who to call. My heart goes out to those people. One day on the job and the next day on the dole. Key cards disabled, badges deactivated, and identities stripped—because in the new normal no one cares what you used to be.

Our business elite robbed us blind and some went to jail. Others who deserved jail didn't get their just desserts. Once upon a time, company CEOs felt a certain level of responsibility to their organization, along with a bond to the people who depended upon them. Those days are gone. Bernard Ebbers of WorldCom, Dennis Kozlowski of Tyco, Richard Scrushy of Healthsouth, Jeffrey Skilling of Enron, and Bernard Madoff of Bernard L. Madoff Investment Securities went to jail. These were the more egregious and unlucky fish. Can you imagine how many didn't get caught? The ones who got lucky or had friends in higher places. Can you even conceive how much they collectively managed to steal? A billion here and billion there. As Everett Dirkson once said, "Sooner or later, it becomes real money."

Our business elite robbed us blind and some did *not* go to jail. I'm talking about the CEOs who found loopholes and workarounds that allowed them to pilfer astonishing amounts of wealth as their companies collapsed around them. Equilar is a blue chip organization that benchmarks executive compensation. They revealed that Angelo Mozillo of Countrywide Financial had take-home pay for 2005-07 of $361.7 million. Richard Fuld pocketed 186.5 million in the last three years of Lehman Brothers' existence.

Kerry Killinger of Washington Mutual took home $36 million in 2005-07. The economy was literally melting all around us, while they took sweetheart deals and payouts with a level of greed that is almost unimaginable. I write this at one o'clock in the morning, sounding cool and clinical, but I feel purple with rage for what this did to you and me. To say I feel your pain is an understatement.

We have outsourced an astonishing number of jobs to other countries, thanks to the cheap labor that's available overseas. Once our CEOs realized an organization's most controllable expense is its workforce and every dollar saved there falls to the bottom line, they've become obsessed with cutting jobs for short term savings. As a result, we Americans manufacture little in the United States. Our technical support calls go to massive centers in India, and heaven knows where else, and every person who picks up your call represents a job that used to be here.

Look around for a moment. Are you driving a foreign made vehicle? Where was your TV set manufactured? Check out your kids' electronic games. Were they made in Chicago? I don't think so—and that's the tip of the iceberg. With the exception of a few pockets of local goods, we no longer make things here.

General Motors declared bankruptcy. Who would ever believe General Motors would be forced to declare bankruptcy? Do you have any idea how big that is? Sadly, as General Motors goes, so goes Detroit. Quoting from a special report in *Time Magazine*, October 5, 2009: "By any quantifiable standard, the city is on life support. Detroit's treasury is $300 million short of the funds needed to provide the barest municipal services. The school system, which six years ago was compelled by the teachers' union to reject a philanthropist's offer of $200 million to build 15 small, independent charter high schools, is in receivership. The murder rate is soaring, and 7 out of 10 remain unsolved. Three years after Katrina devastated New Orleans, unemployment in that city hit a peak of 11 percent. In Detroit, the unemployment rate is 28.9 percent. That's worth spelling out: twenty-eight point nine percent."

Tell me, would your father even recognize this America?

Years ago, a bankrupt General Motors was unimaginable. They say GM at its worst was hemorrhaging almost $55,000 per minute. That's the equivalent of one full size Chevy Suburban every 60 seconds. Every bad deal; every bad car; every million dollars wasted led to this monstrous debacle. The expense accounts, parties, booze, and waste were staggering. Make no mistake about it: we will pay the price of their bankruptcy for a long time.

Obama fired Rick Wagoner. "General Motors Corporation Chairman and CEO Rick Wagoner will step down immediately at the request of the White House." I never met Rick Wagoner, but from a distance, as a car enthusiast and a Rick Wagoner watcher, I always liked him. I viewed him as the quintessential Boy Scout who would make a great neighbor and a trusted friend. Therefore, I took no glee in his departure. On the other hand, he wasn't the right person for the job and hadn't been for many years. GM made cars people didn't want, and it hemorrhaged cash, including $50.7 billion in bailout money. Rumor has it that when GM unveiled the Aztek in 2001, there was only a gasp and then dead silence for this unspeakably ugly car, instantly hated by one and all. How in all that is holy could Wagoner allow a car like this to see the light of day? He should have laid his body in front of it before the image hit the press. Anyone who follows automobile engineering would look at that car and fall to the floor laughing. I remember seeing pictures of that thing at the unveiling and thinking one thing: We are dead.

As you can see, the poor leadership of Wagoner at GM devastated us all. What's worse is the fact that he was forced out by the Obama administration. The president of the United States, in essence, fired a Fortune 500 CEO. That is not only absolutely unprecedented;

it's downright embarrassing. It took an act of government to do what a board of directors should have done a decade ago. The fact that his board didn't remove this sadly ineffective CEO is a glaring example of failed leadership. This board had a moral and fiduciary responsibility to do what was in General Motors' best interest. They proved to be absolutely worthless—cowards of the highest order—rich folks living in exclusive enclaves, conducting business on the golf course. If you think they give a damn about GM, I suggest you rethink your position. If you think they care one iota about your bailout money, or the fact that the U.S. government owns over 60 percent of General Motors as of June 1, 2009 , I suggest you rethink that position as well. Let me rephrase this:

Our government owns nothing. We taxpayers are the owners. It was your money. That money is gone.

U.S Government spends trillions to bail out private industry.

*As quoted from Newsweek, "The equity research division of financial firm Keefe, Bruyette & Wood estimates that the U.S. has spent $3.2 trillion and allocated $10.8 trillion. This includes bailouts financed by the Treasury, the Fed, the FDIC, and HUD."

The jury is still out on the government bailouts Obama provided to the mortgage, financial, automotive, and other sectors. No one is sure what negative financial consequences will result from this massive bailout move. My research shows the number will be somewhere in the trillions. In terms of effectiveness, who can say what life would be like without the bailouts, or how effectively the money was utilized? Ask eleven different economists and you'll get fourteen different answers, so good luck with that. The US deficit just hit $1.4 trillion in September 2010. If you don't find this frightening, you're braver than I am.

---

* http://www.newsweek.com/blogs/wealth-of-nations/2009/04/27/
q-how-much-have-the-bailouts-cost-us-a-all-of-the-above.html

I suspect much of our money went to prop up organizations that are doomed. Perhaps the funds saved a few companies and jobs here and there, but it's a nice way to disguise business models that are no longer viable. Cash is a soothing balm for the dysfunctional and the broken. I believe the bailout money was, for the most part, spent in ways so inefficient and wasteful they're beyond our comprehension.

In the world of high finance and big government, much has happened in a short time. Financially speaking, it's all bad. Now is the time for us as a people to move on and look forward, because if we can adapt, change, and persevere, the best may be ahead of us. Creating a new and better world should be the personal objective of every one of us. The first step in doing this is to remain forward-thinking and hopeful.

Chapter 5
The Underbelly of Corporate America

*And sometimes I actually start to think human life is
just as cheap to corporate America as animal life,
so long as there are big profits to be made.*

—*Tom Scholz*

*I*want to be nice. I want to start out on the right foot, on a
positive, uplifting note about life in corporate America. Let me
struggle for civility in the hope of providing a fair and balanced
commentary.

For openers, let me say I'm sure many corporate enclaves foster
growth, creativity, and a sense of real purpose. They employ honest
people pulling together for the common good; well-meaning
people trying to do what's right for their fellow employees inside
the organization, as they attempt to be good corporate citizens in
the community. If you keep your head down, do your job, and try to
get along, things may work out fine for you in such a corporation.
Perhaps you'll land in a good, decent place to work. Fifteen to 20
percent of companies reflect this almost Utopian ideal. Don't let me
discourage you from pursuing a dream job in corporate America.
Perhaps you can use your sphere of influence to change your
corporation in some small way for the good. I applaud you for that.

There you have it. I'm done. I tried, but that's the best I can do. Now let's move on to the vast majority of corporations in America: ugly, brutish places where power struggles are more important than productivity, and *who* you know matters infinitely more than *what* you know. Understanding how to get along is critical here. Be careful of what you say, what you do, and who and what you endorse. Form the wrong loyalties and you'll find swift punishment meted out by those whose sensibilities, monstrous egos, and political agendas you offended. Do you want to be in the loop about details of an important project? Do you want to ever attend another important meeting related to your career and your responsibilities? Yes, you say? Then be careful how you play the game. Let me give you a quick tip: if the day ever comes when eye contact is suddenly diminished and people stop talking with you, then you're in big trouble.

Corporate America is a great place if you want to climb to the top of whatever pile happens to interest you. If you have no problem viewing going to work as going to war, there's a place in corporate America just for you.

If you fall into the category of angry bully, you'll love corporate America. Possess a tendency toward malevolence, coupled with a Machiavellian outlook on life? Welcome home, baby!

Hoping to show all those bastards from high school a thing or two? Looking for the opportunity to kick some serious ass? If you're a proficient kicker with a title and a little talent, you'll thrive in this environment. If you epitomize Napoleon, thrive on a diet of passive aggressive behavior, and love to win at any cost, you'll flourish in corporate America. Show me an angry, short man with enough talent to get by, and I'll show you a perfect player for this sad game. It's like mother's milk to them. Are you misogynistic and a big fan of buff guys with golf shirts? This job is for you. Are you good at holding a grudge based upon a perceived slight that was so unintentional, so long ago, and so devoid of meaning that you're still angry but can't remember why? Your cubicle is waiting. Welcome home to corporate America.

Angry women can also prosper in corporate America. Do you want to show all your friends their lives are no better than yours? Are you obsessed with being a mom, a wife, and an executive? Did you miss going to the prom? Been in a bad mood since college? Well, come on down, because the coffee's hot and they're waiting just for you.

If you don't fall into any of the psychotic profiles above, life in these environs might be a problem for you. I suggest you carefully consider the following before you make your deal with the devil:

1. There's an excellent chance you won't enjoy your job if you're reluctant to enter the game of down and dirty office politics and not willing to play it every single day.

2. You won't even be a serious player if you think the job is about survival of the smartest as opposed to survival of the snarkiest. As an aside, this is exactly why so many corporate CEOs seem incompetent when they're forced to speak publicly about whatever odious event has taken place within their ranks. Few know what to say; few know how to say it; and few should be CEOs in the first place.

3. If you're looking for an organization where you can do good work, speak your mind in an honest and forthright manner, and let the pieces fall where they may, corporate America may not be the ideal place to ply your craft.

Do you think I'm exaggerating? Do some research and draw your own conclusions. If you want to go back a bit, read *Up the Organization*[2] by Robert Townsend and see what it was like back in the day. Want to see more recent information and opinion? Read Dominique Browning's lovely memoir, *Slow Love: How I Lost*

My Job, Put on My Pajamas and Found Happiness.[3] For a different perspective, watch the movie *"Up in the Air"* for a sad, yet realistic, take on just how depressing this life can be.

One of the biggest issues for corporate workers is the endless pressure to keep the head count down and hire as few full time employees as possible. Who comes, who goes, and how much work is on everyone's plate is just the tip of the iceberg. This downward pressure on head count exists because payroll always takes a large chunk of the corporate budget—a fixed overhead that must be paid every week. And, it's the single most controllable expense in the organization. What manager could resist tinkering with it?

Corporate America always wants to save money to keep stockholders happy. How could we achieve that end? Cut the electric bill or get cheaper computers? Probably not viable solutions. Stop giving away free coffee? That would only save a few pennies. Cut personal days and reduce benefits? You might save a few bucks here, but honestly these solutions aren't big enough.

Wait! What about cutting jobs? We could stop replacing employees who leave. What about doing more work with fewer people? That seems fair. The salaried folks can move faster, come in earlier, and stay later. They will burn out, you say? No problem; they can be replaced.

Honestly now, what are current employees going to do if you work them harder? Complain? Employees should thank their lucky stars they have a job in the first place.

Wait! If getting rid of a few people is good, what about getting rid of large groups of people—entire departments? Is that not even better? Hello, outsourcing!

What about moving certain functions to other countries? How about bringing on contractors through lowest bid vendor management systems? That way we won't have to pay benefits, and the accounting department can work their magic to dazzle our shareholders. Think about a labor supply with no vacation days, no sick days, nothing resembling job security, and no upward mobility. These contractors are temporary and expendable. These pseudo-employees can be turned on and off like a water faucet. Work a day, get paid for a day. Work a week, get paid for a week. Day laborers in a jacket and a tie. Don't like the way one looked at you this morning? Got his coffee before you got yours? She suggested another way of handling that project? (Even worse, she was right, but it made you look bad in front of the group.) Go ahead, make that call, because it will make you feel good all day long.

"Joe?" This is Frank. Please make today Mary's last day."

"Okay. Will do"

"Thanks. Bye."

Now that's good living in corporate America. Lunch anyone?

Let's talk about hiring. No longer is hiring a priority in corporate America. They'll tell you they want to hire the best and brightest, but it's only lip service. Sure, companies put up cute websites with videos of happy employees who describe how they adore their jobs. That's corporate spin. Pure malarkey—designed to please an often times clueless CEO and stockholders who really don't care if their employees live or die. Are there exceptions? Sure, but not many.

Let's Take a Look Behind the Scenes

In the traditional hiring model, a new employee enters into an agreement with an organization that is, in some ways, akin to marriage. An employment agreement is a recognized legal arrangement in the United States, across Europe,* and in many other civilized countries across the globe. The legal and cost issues surrounding FTEs (full time employees) are major reasons corporations try to avoid hiring.

---

* In most of Europe they're much stricter than we are about separating from an employee. Just try to lay off a worker in Germany.

If a company hires a FTE, they'll be paying benefits that may equal 30 percent of the new hire's compensation package. They also pay multiple taxes to the government for each worker. Many employees are protected by age, race, or unions, so an organization has the added burden of how to get rid of these FTEs if they no longer need their services. Why not avoid all this hassle and get by with contract or outsourced labor?

Can you see why corporate America is slowly moving out of the business of FTEs? Why own when you can rent? Can you see why finding a full-time position in corporate America has become increasingly difficult? In spite of all this, even the most reluctant corporation must sometimes take the plunge and hire another FTE. But why does it take so long for them to make a decision? Why must you do a phone screen, wait, get an interview, wait another three weeks, interview again, and still you get no real answer? Why do the people in power take so long to make a decision?

This, dear reader, is a complex question, and the answer varies from one industry or company to the next. The bottom line is, few people in corporate America wish to actually look the hiring team in the face and say, "I recommend we hire this person, and I intend to do so." Such a bold statement runs counter to the usual culture, where no one takes ownership of any decision.

To actually accept individual responsibility takes a level of intestinal fortitude seldom seen in corporate America. As JFK said, "Success has a million fathers, but failure is an orphan."

No one wants to take responsibility for a bad hiring decision. That's why there are so many committees and endless meetings. No one in corporate America wants to be the one to raise a hand when a senior level person asks the worst and most damming question of all: "Who the hell hired that person?" (If the senior executive asking that question happened to be the one who actually made the hire, I strongly suggest you do not point that out.)

So the hiring process drags on, and you wait. The hiring team vacillates as they discuss candidates. Headhunters call with promises of even better candidates than those the team is already considering. Now agency candidates are tossed into the hiring process, which means tacking on another ninety days. As the person in the interviewing loop, you climb the walls, waiting for any kind of feedback. You struggle not to seem desperate, because hiring managers can smell desperation from a hundred yards. This is a game of "hurry up and wait." The game of, "Can you come in tomorrow and meet with Phil? Can you be here at 8:00?"

Then you wait and still hear nothing. God forbid you call them. God forbid you tell them they look like absolute idiots who can't even employ the brains required to make a hire. That would be death. Your death. You're right, of course, but you send them another thank you e-mail and you wait.

The hiring team has a few candidates they really like for the position, but they haven't yet uncovered the "perfect candidate" and wonder why they can't identify that person. We all know the perfect candidate is mythical, but let's explore this further. The perfect candidate fantasy can be a nightmare in a down economy. Flawed corporate logic sounds like this: "With so many people unemployed, the perfect candidate has to be out there, so we'll keep looking until we find that person."

This thought process is akin to a person looking for the perfect mate: another mythical creature. So the hiring team continues to look and look some more. They make slight changes to the profile of the position for reasons unknown, and this sets them back another sixty days. More headhunters descend, as members of the hiring team bicker about the exact requirements for the position. Words are debated, semantics examined and dissected. What exactly do we mean by "manage the process?" Does that mean the person will manage the process from a perspective relating to strategic overview, or more from an operational and vendor compliance angle? More conversation. More phone screens. More interviews as you wait for an answer.

I'll stop here, because I can't present anymore of this ugliness and frightening ineptitude. Let's imagine I'm on the inside. I'd do what I do best: get everyone in a room and tell them nicely this is a problem and we need to solve it now. That we can't take a year to fill a position and call it a critical position. It can't be critical if it's open for a year, because that makes no sense. If it's critical, who's doing the job right now? No one? "Then it isn't critical!" I scream silently while trying not to pull my hair out.

I ask gently, in a soothing, dulcet tone, "If someone is doing this job now, who is it, and why should we change things?"

I get blank stares. No real answers emerge. Then people stare at the floor. My inner self-talk goes into silent scream mode again. "Folks, you look like fools and the entire organization is watching. Do you want to do this for another six months or will you allow me to drive the process and help you to make this happen? Do you really want to be discussing this at Christmas time?"

I want to rage at their incompetence, their gall, and their fear of doing their jobs. The veins in my head throb. I get coffee.

I know I will make this happen because I'm good at what I do. The warm, sweet liquid clears my head, and I begin again the process of meeting with all the team members and hammering out a plan.

Let's take this down a notch, and I'll tell you a story that happened just last week.

I spoke with a life sciences client who's been searching for a Director of Quality for a medical devices company for almost 18 months. They are a train wreck; no matter who they interview, they can't seem to pick someone and make the hire.

Just imagine this? The company has been looking for a director/senior level person almost two years, they're still going through first round phone screening and interviews, and they keep winding up back on square one. Honestly, this makes me purple with anger.

Let's look at another aspect of corporate American while I take a few deep breaths.

The Myth of Stability

Many people seek a job in corporate America to find stability. With a stable, salaried job they can buy a house in a good neighborhood, own a reliable car, be assured of quality healthcare, and raise a family.

That's how things used to work. I urge you *not* to set the same expectations your fathers and mothers had when it comes to stability and job security. The last few years have demonstrated that entire companies can simply disappear, through no fault of the loyal employees who worked in the trenches. The new normal has transformed the notion of corporate stability into a myth.

I believe Harvey MacKay said it best: "Beware of loving the organization because it will never love you back." You can take that advice to the bank.

The Myth of Responsibility

Author and journalist Ambrose Bierce aptly defined a corporation as "an ingenious device for obtaining profit without taking individual responsibility." He speaks to the simple fact that no one in corporate America is responsible for anything. Let me give you an example. If a car company built an automobile containing a dangerous flaw and released it to the public, would someone go to jail for the deaths and injuries they caused? Of course not. Has anyone at Toyota served jail time? Has anyone associated with the Gulf oil spill set foot in prison? Have you ever seen a CEO go to jail after admitting a horrible tragedy occurred on his watch, and that he holds himself accountable? Not in a million years. Wall Street punishes the guilty for a moment, but in the end no one cares. Corporate America is all about profit, and we live in a capitalistic society.

Someone who read this manuscript slapped the pages down and asked me, "How do you have the nerve to write stuff like this? What if no one ever hires you again? What if they sue you? What if this is read by the wrong people?"

I sat quietly and looked at her as she continued, "How can you even write this as though it's gospel?"

Perhaps you're asking the same questions. Here's my answer: It doesn't matter what I write. Corporate America is not human. Corporate America doesn't have a soul or feelings that can be hurt. Corporate America is a legal entity, and that allows it to act with absolute impunity, without caring whether you and I live or die. Corporate America operates with a crowd mentality that has no compassion for individuals. The CFO who'd stop in the rain to help you change a flat tire today will lay you off in a heartbeat tomorrow. How will you pay your bills? Not his problem—just business as usual.

Capitalism, like free will, comes with a price tag. Someone in the know once said:

"The goal of life in corporate America is to get out of it."

Think about that. Think about it long and hard, because it was said by someone who really understands corporate America.

Chapter 6

Active and Passive Candidates: Lord Help the Unemployed

> *"That's the problem with unemployment —you wake up and you are on the job."*
>
> —Laurie Bick

Active and Passive Job Candidates

I know what you're thinking. What on earth are active and passive candidates? I almost don't want to tell you, because this phenomenon is so disturbing and unfair that you may find it hard to believe the concept exists.

Let's start with a working definition of active candidates: folks who demonstrate their desire for new employment through involvement with job boards, completing online applications, and overt statements in blogs, associations, user groups, Twitter, LinkedIn, and Facebook. They may be unemployed, or employed and seeking a better opportunity. Regardless of the reason, they're out there hustling, trying to get ahead in life. I know this is true, because I'm one of these people.

Passive candidates are currently employed, not seeking another position. They may be hustlers in temperament, but they aren't looking. They don't have resumes posted on the job boards, nor do they fill out online applications. Hence the term *passive*.

What's the problem with this scenario, you ask? People who want a job will find it, and those who aren't looking will simply stay put.

Not quite that simple

Over the last four or five years, the recruiting community has been pushing an agenda that makes active candidates seem less desirable then passive candidates. Ugly and discriminatory as it is, let me clarify this for you. Many so-called "thought leaders" in the recruiting field advise employers to avoid hiring active candidates, because these people are unemployed, and obviously not "A" players. If they were any good they'd already have a job—and why hire a person who isn't any good?

Why hire a person who's unemployed? That is twisted logic, but it's real, and it's out there. Perhaps you've gone back to read the last statement again, because you can't believe what I just said. Folks, it's true. I couldn't make up anything this bizarre.

But, I urge you to do your own research and see what's being written about active and passive candidates. This will help you understand the twisted logic espoused by many hiring "experts" who sell recruiting services to corporate America. It's prejudicial. It is insidious. But like it or not, this is the mindset you're fighting every day as an active candidate. Many hiring managers will look at your resume, see you've been out of work for an extended period of time, and pass you by because if you were any good, you wouldn't need a job.

Do you feel rage at this? Do you feel angry that a company to whom you've applied for a position might pass you over because your last position was with a company that laid you off because of declining business conditions? Can you see the bitter paradox in the fact that the reason you were laid off had nothing to do with your capabilities, and yet it's still held against you?

How does it feel to be screwed over by corporate America not once, but twice? "Thanks and thanks again," as I call it.

Screwed first by the company that laid you off, and then by companies who won't look twice at your application because you're not working. Can it get any worse? *The Huffington Post dated 1-14-11 entitled How Employers Weed Out Unemployed Job Applicants, Others, Behind The Scenes, the author says: A 53-year-old executive recruiter named Nick, who asked that his full name be withheld to protect his job, told Huffington Post he has worked for major U.S. staffing firms since 1990. As an industry insider, Nick said, he became privy to the many ways companies and staffing firms sidestep labor laws. "There's a lot of dirty stuff going on, a lot of hush-hush discrimination, I can assure you," he said. "As a recruiter, you get an HR director on the phone, and they tell you point blank, 'We want somebody in this age bracket, or this particular gender, currently has a job. We don't want to see a resume from anyone who's not working.' It happens all the time."

Let's take a deep breath and try to understand why active and passive candidates have become a growing issue. Back in the days when recruiters spoke of a War for Talent, we competed for certain hard-to-find candidates who had specialized skills. Many of these candidates, but not all, were technologists. We headhunters touted our ability to entice highly specialized candidates to venture out and meet with our clients. If the specialist we submitted was hired, we received a fee. A big fee. They called us headhunters, because we'd go inside a corporation and lure passive candidates away from their firms, delivering them to our clients' doorsteps. There's nothing wrong with this practice, and it's especially effective for positions where there aren't enough good candidates to go around.

---

* http://www.huffingtonpost.com/2011/01/14/unemployed-job-applicants-discrimination_n_809010.html

Unfortunately, this thinking invaded the philosophies of corporate hiring managers and those in HR by creating a built-in prejudice toward active candidates. In simple terms, the thinking in corporate America often goes like this:

"Active candidate: bad.

Passive candidate: good."

This is a slap in the face to all who are victims of this intractable recession.

What can you do to battle this corporate mindset? Not a lot, since you don't sit around the table when resumes are presented and read. My advice is to push hard for an interview and don't be afraid to discuss why you're unemployed. You have a story to tell, so go ahead and tell it, because getting laid off in this economy is nothing to be ashamed of.

Out of work for 18 months? Out of work for one day? Be proud of what you accomplished and discuss it in your interview. Focus on what you can do to bring great value to the position for which you're interviewing.

Keep reading, because the following chapters will show you how to get your foot inside the door and overcome these passive versus active candidate issues.

Chapter 7

Ask Not What Networking Can Do For You

"It's the oldest, corniest piece of advice in the world but it still works. The strongest networks are built on friendship. Be a friend not only to the people in your network, but to the people who matter the most to the people in your network."

—Harvey Mackay

*N*etworking means many things. It may be picking up the phone and saying hello or texting and e-mailing an old friend, or attending events specifically designed to help you meet others. Networking can take place on social sites like Facebook, or business sites such as LinkedIn. Networking can be tied to forums, through blogging, or via online venues emerging every day. Video is now popular, as it connects to every conceivable type of smart phone. The future possibilities for networking are absolutely endless.

In the most fundamental definition, networking is outreach to others—an attempt to stay connected and remain in touch. It's ongoing communication with what has become a fragile milieu of friends, associates, former coworkers, and complete strangers. Networking allows each of us to try and get what we need from others without becoming a pest or driving people insane.

Not long ago, networking was less complicated. Business friends chatted back and forth anywhere from weekly to once a year, just to keep up on the latest news and stay connected. "How's your daughter and are you still playing golf? Need anything?" Followed by a shared laugh and a promise to get together soon. A more personal and civilized type of networking was explored by Harvey MacKay in his landmark book *Swim With the Sharks Without Getting Eaten Alive.*[4] This book is required reading for everyone who wants to make something happen and learn from the master. Things have changed since the book was first published, and now Harvey is on Facebook, LinkedIn, Twitter, and probably a host of other places where he can do all his fans a world of good.

Because good networking is a key element to a successful job search, the way you conduct yourself is vitally important. In recent years the game has become high speed and low touch as we network with people we barely know.

Going one step further, many of those with whom we network are people we've never met and perhaps never will meet but can be very important to us. I have a couple of online friends I've never met in person or spoken with, yet I'd drop everything in a heartbeat to help them.

Networking has unwritten rules of engagement, and folks who violate them can be left out in the cold. These rules call for a delicate, tactful approach to achieve results. Let's look at nine talking points to get your head into this game.

Pay It Forward

The time to network is always now. Gaining connections and adding new people to your contact community is a positive move. The best way to start on the right foot is to go out there and offer to help others before you ask for assistance. The logic behind this is simple: Everyone is looking for something. They either want something for themselves or for their kids, a spouse, or a friend. This mutual need is fine, because as a society we all move forward when we recognize our interdependence. No one succeeds alone.

Society prospers when we spend twice as much time offering help than we spend asking for help.

> In the broadest possible way, I suggest you look at networking as a bank account. Every time you help someone, you're adding funds to your account. Each time you ask for help, you make a withdrawal.

I suggest you do whatever you can to keep your bank account balance as high as possible and make withdrawals only as needed. I strongly encourage you to think before you make requests of anyone, especially those who are nearest and dearest.

When considering a significant withdrawal, use the email rule that seems to work so well: wait 24 hours before you hit the send button. If you truly need something today, you'll probably need it tomorrow as well. So unless someone is bleeding, spend one day thinking before you make the request. If after 24 hours, you decide to move forward with the request, do it with care and tact. And remember that everyone's time is tight and fewer words are more effective than a long, endless missive. Unfortunately, many people who network don't submit to the idea of paying it forward, and that will be their loss in terms of effectiveness and results.

Keep Your Expectations Low

You can't imagine why your old friend Phil hasn't gotten back to you? Such is life, and the sooner you adjust your expectations, the better off you'll be. Most of the time, people act in their own self-interest, and no matter how desperate you feel, your outreach will have to wait until that person is ready to deal with your request. As the saying goes, "Since when does poor planning on your part constitute an emergency on mine?" We all need to be patient while networking and understand that even our best buddies will disappoint us sooner or later. That's the nature of life.

When you reach out, the objective is to do it once—and that's the end. Do you know someone well, with a long-term sense of connection and a history together? Great! If she doesn't respond to your query, call and see if she's okay. Please note I'm not suggesting you call to ask why she didn't get back to you, because that is too self-serving.

I could go on for a full page about the sense of entitlement some of us feel. Other people don't owe you a living, so don't expect handouts—even if you think you deserve them. Are you tempted to write a scathing note along the lines of, "Thanks for nothing"? Don't do it! You'll embarrass yourself and lose any goodwill you've built up with that person, forever.

Suppose she was getting ready to grant your favor the moment your nasty email came in? Perhaps she's been on vacation, or ill. Maybe her cat died. You have no idea what's going on with the other person. Here's how Victoria Strauss blogged about an aspiring writer who asked for help.[5]

"So a week goes by, and just as I'm thinking that I really have to sit down and give this writer a thoughtful answer, I get a nasty note from him implying that I've wasted his time and asking me to at least tell him why I found his work so offensive I couldn't be bothered to respond. Now, maybe when I received his plot summary I should have dashed off a note letting him know that it'd be several days before I could reply. On the other hand, it's not like anyone is paying me to answer requests for advice from total strangers. Given that he was asking me for a favor, I assumed that he was willing to be patient. I wrote back to tell him so, upon which he informed me that he wasn't going to kiss my ass just to get my help. Ooooookay"

This bad tempered writer is lucky Victoria Strauss didn't publish his name and email address. The moral of the story? If you ask for something and get a negative response or no answer at all, chalk it up to business as usual and move on with your life.

Specifics Required

When it comes to sharing your request or need, please be specific. People can't help you if they don't know what you want. Be sure you're clear and leave no room for misunderstanding. Simply requesting help to find a job won't cut it. That's way too broad. People may want to help, but have no idea what you need from them. As a result, they do nothing. You must do the work and be definite about what you want.

For example, if you want someone to act as a reference, provide that person with a copy of your resume, a brief description of the types of jobs you've applied for, and the names of those who might be calling. Stay in touch with them as the months pass, giving updates on your progress. And remember to express your thanks in appropriate ways.

Don't beat around the bush. This isn't the time for passive aggressive statements, such as: "If only I could find someone to help with my resume." Don't hint at what you need—be direct: "Bob, I wonder if you could spare an hour to go over my resume and give me some tips. I'll bring the coffee." Also let the other person know how much time you expect from them, because time is a valuable commodity.

Always Answer

Some people believe God answers all prayers, but sometimes the answer is "no." If that's your answer to someone who asks you for help, do not ignore them. No matter if you're traveling, struggling with a project, or leaving for Hong Kong—answer them, and answer quickly. Your answer doesn't need to be long or detailed, but being prompt is a good thing, and others will remember you for it. Ignoring those who are attempting to network is bad karma—something we can all do without. Furthermore, saying *no* by avoiding the question is a poor way to do business—and bad manners. If you must say no, do it nicely and sweetly, but be sure to go ahead and say it. People will understand and forgive you if you can't fulfill their request, but they may not forget the slap in the face you give them by not responding.

Give Value

Value has a number of definitions, but in this context think of it as a type of worth or usefulness to the other person involved.

Value can take many forms: introductions, information, insight, and ideas. The surest arbiter of real value lies with the person to whom it's presented. He or she is the ultimate judge of what you're offering.

Providing real value can mean a variety of things to those in need. For example, it might be recommending a website, providing a link, a guest blog, or an introduction. It can come in the form of ten minutes on the phone listening to someone who needs to vent. Use your listening skills to determine exactly what the other person needs and wants from you. Don't be in such a hurry to respond that you miss the real question. Value is king. Give it to as many people as you can, as often as possible. You will be remembered.

Don't Sell, and Don't Spam

Networking and selling are like water and gasoline—they don't mix. Many LinkedIn account holders specifically request no selling. Ignoring these guidelines is a bad idea. Networking is a delicate business, because at some point you may be asking for something— an introduction, information that's usually kept quiet, the chance to get to talk with someone who usually isn't available, and other types of value-based activity. These requests take time from the person to whom you're reaching out. Be careful you don't put them in an uncomfortable position. Remember: no selling, and no spam—ever. Unless you're involved in the type of networking group where you're allowed to sell, it's in your best interest to avoid selling. I can't think of a better way to burn all those bridges you've carefully built.

Understand Rejection

Rejection is part of life, and more often than not it isn't personal. Let's take LinkedIn as an example. This is a powerful business tool that helps many people. On the other hand, it's also a place that can use a lot of your valuable time, and the time of the people to whom you reach out. Some people may only be second or third connections who barely know you. Often they won't have patience for requests and introductions to others with whom they're linked. If this is the case, don't be surprised if they won't help you. I suggest you understand that person's position and try to help yourself some other way. Translation: getting upset is a waste of time.

As an example, if someone on LinkedIn asked me to arrange an introduction to a third person, I'd evaluate the request and ask myself a few important questions. First, I'd have to make a judgment call and ask myself: "Will this person be comfortable with my LinkedIn request?" Secondly, "Is the person making a LinkedIn request of me someone I trust? How well do I know him?" I can't over emphasize the trust factor, because the last thing I want in my life is to get an e-mail or voice mail that says, "Thanks for sending that turkey my way." If that happens, I feel burned and embarrassed.

This is business, where people must protect their reputations. I can't afford to be embarrassed, and neither can you. Please be tactful and sensitive to those of whom you make a request. And be mindful when considering the requests of others.

Givers versus Takers

Be known as one who helps, not someone who constantly asks for help. I used to have a coworker who'd call me like clockwork, six or seven times a year. The calls always came on Sunday evening, just to shoot the breeze and talk about business and life. At the end of the conversation, he would always say, without missing a beat, "Howard, is there anything I can do for you?" I'll never forget him and our conversations.

I was truly blessed to have the friendship of this world-class networker who played the game so well that I didn't even know he was doing it. Years later, I finally had the brains to ask, "Is there anything I can do for you?"

This is the type of networker you wish to become. You need to be seen as the person who's always there to help and support others first, and ask favors as a distant second. I think I know what some of you are thinking. What happens if you do more favors for the world than people do for you? Absolutely nothing bad will happen! You'll become known as a good person who helps others. You'll be recognized as someone who can be counted upon for support; one of your profession's darlings; a person who's a giver rather than a taker. Honestly, is that such a bad legacy?

Manage Your Online Content:
You are what you post

In this age of networking we can find background information on almost anyone, from people we know to folks we've never met. Sometimes that creates a false sense of intimacy. If several thousand people follow me on Twitter and read my blog, do I know them? In a broad sense they're my friends, but I doubt they'd like me to drop in for dinner. You might say our social policies and business etiquette haven't been able to keep up with this new technology. We need to remember we're only connected by the tenuous bond of the Internet.

In this Internet age, we each have two personas: the person who shakes hands, goes out for lunch with colleagues, and makes telephone calls—and that mythical, online person who can be accessed around the globe.

We need to always present ourselves in a professional manner if we want to be taken seriously, and managing our online content is the place to begin. The rule of thumb is simple: take everything seriously, because you never know who's watching. Many employers check prospective employees on Facebook and other social media before making a job offer. This should be common knowledge, but apparently job seekers haven't absorbed the message.

> Idiot pictures of you and your buddies, half naked, drunk, and hanging your tongues out, will not help you in the professional world.

Ditch the swimwear and underwear photos, along with dirty jokes and bathroom humor.

Search engines allow employers to scour all manner of digital dirt to vet employees. Online profile company Ziggs.com CEO Tim DeMello fired an intern after he discovered a note on the intern's Facebook profile saying that while at Ziggs he would "spend most of my days screwing around on IM talking to my friends and getting paid for it."

A report by Harris Interactive for Careerbuilder.com[6] found that most employers use Facebook for online detective work, followed by LinkedIn and MySpace. In addition, 7 percent followed job candidates on Twitter. Thirty-five percent of employers reported finding content on social networking sites that caused them not to hire a candidate. The top examples include:

- Candidate posted provocative or inappropriate photographs or information - 53 percent.
- Candidate posted content about drinking or using drugs - 44 percent
- Candidate bad-mouthed a previous employer, co-workers or clients - 35 percent
- Candidate showed poor communication skills - 29 percent
- Candidate made discriminatory comments - 26 percent

- Candidate lied about qualifications - 24 percent
- Candidate shared confidential information from previous employer - 20 percent

Fourteen percent of employers have disregarded a candidate because the candidate sent a message using an emoticon such as a smiley face, while 16 percent dismissed a candidate for using text language, such as GR8 (great) in an e-mail or job application.

The professional world is watching. Did you think those pictures were private and strangers had no right to access them? The Internet is public domain, and that means for public consumption. Do you have a job interview next week? You probably don't want the hiring managers to see that at age 37 you're still partying at keggers on the beach, holding your favorite beer and looking wasted. Smarten up and expunge the personal photos before you lose something that's important to you. **Consider yourself warned.** Never put anything personal on the Internet unless you're willing to have the Presentation Nuns give it a once-over. Never badmouth former employers and fellow employees. That's the kiss of death.

If verbal content is a problem, clean up your act. Get rid of uncouth language, tasteless jokes, and heavy political content. If you're blogging and have issues with grammar and punctuation, ask someone to edit your blogs before you post them.

Google your name at least once a month to see what turns up. You may be surprised where your name is lurking on the Internet. Be selective about your associations, and monitor comments made on your blog and other sites. Keep your content positive, on both a personal and professional level.

The good news is, you can also use the Internet to enhance your image and strengthen your chances of finding a job. You can use professional sites like LinkedIn, Facebook, or Twitter to form relationships with other professionals and with recruiters. Without bragging, you can highlight your accomplishments inside your profession and in your personal life. Show your solid communication skills by writing intelligent, thoughtful material that will help others. Avoid slang and don't use text language that makes you sound like a teenager.

The best way to approach online content is to pretend your next employer is looking over your shoulder, wondering if you'd be a good fit for their organization.

Chapter 8

Headhunters: A Crash Course

"They are a tribe with their own language. They are expert trappers, but also excel at fishing expeditions. And at first encounter in Headhunters: Matchmaking in the Labor Market, they seem friendly enough. But would you like to meet one in a dark boardroom?"
—Nina C. Ayoub
Chronicle of Higher Education, March 22, 2002

*E*xplained in the simplest terms, headhunters are employment recruiters, but not all recruiters are headhunters. Headhunters are utilized by organizations and companies to help them find candidates, often executives, but increasingly senior level technologists and engineers at both the individual contributor and management levels.

Headhunters are gatekeepers in the world of employment, and they often get a bad rap because people don't understand the relationship. These are some of the things I've heard people say:

- Headhunters never call you back.

- Headhunters don't care if you live or die—they're just in it for the money.

- Headhunters are totally insensitive.
- Headhunters don't understand (or care) what I want.

Negative comments about headhunters are endless, contradictory, true, and false, all at the same time. The truth is, your opinion about headhunters will be formed by your needs, the specific headhunter with whom you work, the economy, and the overall job market. Sometimes a headhunter will be your best asset in a job search. Other times, he can get in the way instead of helping.

The average headhunter is trying to balance the needs of three parties, each of whom has complicated political, emotional, and financial requirements. This is no easy task, and he seldom makes everyone happy. Let's look at eight talking points that can help you work effectively with headhunters and create a win-win outcome.

Headhunters Work for the Client

Headhunters work for the client, because that's who signs the check. Headhunters are paid by their clients on a contingency basis, or on retainer. In rare cases, headhunters will indeed work for you, as a hired agent to help manage and drive your job search, but that's a different scenario. I need you to remember that a headhunter will act in his own self-interest above the interests of others, and therein lies the misunderstanding some people experience.

Headhunters do not work for you. That's the long and short of it.

Naturally, we want to keep our clients satisfied to encourage repeat business. If a headhunter placed a candidate whose compensation was $80,000 at a 20 percent fee of base compensation, that means the headhunter will receive a check for $16,000 about thirty days after that person's starting date. If the fee was 25 percent, the check would be $20,000. Can you see why it's a good idea to keep clients happy? Instead of hopping from one client to the next, most headhunters want to collect a fee and then get an immediate assignment to fill another position—or five assignments at once. The real money in headhunting comes from repeat business, and finding a steady client is our dream. Does that help you understand why the client's needs become a headhunter's and top priority?

They'll Call You If They Have Something

This is a simple formula: headhunters will be in touch with you if they have a reason to be in touch. If they have nothing for you, in most all cases, they won't call. This doesn't reflect an insensitive attitude—it's business. Back in the day when I was crazy aggressive, as opposed to normally aggressive, I would crawl over broken glass to get you on the phone if I needed to set up an interview with one of my clients. Believe me, if a headhunter has a reason to call you, the phone will ring. Calling the headhunter just to "check in" has little value. Try to remember that just because your phone is quiet doesn't mean nothing is happening behind the scenes.

Headhunters Are Not Career Counselors

If you expect a headhunter to help with your resume, answer your questions about interviewing, and do other career counselor types of duties, you won't have much luck.

> Expecting a headhunter to coach you through all aspects of the job hunt is unrealistic.

The one exception to this rule is if the headhunter decides to prep you for an interview with the client because he or she understands the job inside and out. If you pay attention, the headhunter can tell you what's important to the client and how to best present your qualifications for the position. Every headhunter hopes to have the client fall in love with you and make an offer; we know a well prepped candidate has the best chance of generating interest.

Help the Headhunter Help You

If you want a headhunter to help you, the best thing you can do is let him know who you are, what you've done, and how you can benefit his clients. He needs to fully understand your background, strengths, and accomplishments. For example, if you're an environmental engineer who's a cut above the rest of the profession, let the headhunter know you're more than a science geek with a master's degree: you can manage projects, and your clients adore you.

"Get me in front of your client and they'll see I'm not just an engineer, but a business developer who brought in over $4 million in revenue to my last company for the price of a few client dinners."

If you want a headhunter's client to love you, tell the headhunter exactly why they should. You'll get better results and more interviews. Helping the headhunter understand you're not only qualified, but exemplary, is vital to both of you.

The Headhunter Is There to Fill a Position, Not Get You a Job

I'm stunned by how many people ask me if I can get them a job. Usually, I can't. However, they can work with me if appropriate— and if they do what's required. I can prep them and deliver them to the door; after that, they're on their own. I'll say it again, with emphasis: *the headhunter is not there to get you a job.* His role is to fill a position for his client's organization. If you're selected for a position, then it seems the headhunter *did* find you a job—but that wasn't his primary objective. The bottom line? You got yourself the job.

Close the Door and Be Quiet

Let me frame the question before you ask: "What should I do if a headhunter calls me?"

There you are, hard at work, and life is just fine. The call comes out of the blue, and here's the conversation:

"Hello, my name is Howard Adamsky, and I'm calling from an executive search and consulting company just west of Boston. One of my clients has a very interesting opportunity for a Director of Regulatory Affairs. Can you talk for a moment?" (This is, word for word, exactly what I would say to you.) I get all types of reactions: Fear, happiness, shock, laughter, and sometimes absolute silence.

If a headhunter calls, the best policy is to close your door, be friendly, and chat about the opportunity for a few moments. No one is asking you to take the job, because no one has even offered it to you. He's checking your availability and interest. If you aren't available, perhaps you can refer someone who is looking for a position. If you're absolutely unable to talk at that moment, suggest a time when you'll be free to discuss the opportunity.

> A special word for those who become angry with headhunter calls. Don't do that. Really now, smarten up. That phone call means you're respected and in demand. Don't be upset when the calls come in—be upset when they stop coming.

Have the Relationship Before You Need It

Headhunters can be a funny bunch. They don't like to feel used—treated well when you're on the prowl for a position, but ignored the rest of the time. If the day comes where you're seeking a job, for any reason, it's wise to have a preexisting relationship with a headhunter. Actually, you should cultivate several of these relationships.

One of the best ways to leverage the relationship is to provide the headhunter with value—especially if there's no upside for you. Doing this person a good turn is money in the bank. For example, if you discover a large company will need twenty project managers for a large government contract, and they need them fast, can you see the value in making a quick call to the headhunter and sharing that information? Can you see that call might take you five minutes? Now imagine the value of having this person on your side if you ever need a position. Once again, I advise you to develop the relationships before you need them.

Don't Ask

Do not start your relationship by asking about the fee. This is proprietary information between the client and headhunter. Also, don't ask questions about other candidates for the position. Of course there will be other candidates, because each client wants to interview a number of people and get a strong feel for who's out there, plus the level of talent they can get. Instead of worrying about the competition, focus on presenting yourself in the best light. That's the number one thing you can do for yourself, the headhunter, and the client.

Headhunters Differ

As stated, most headhunters work outside the walls of corporate America, acting as third parties. Most are paid a fee only when they "make the hit" by placing a candidate with one of their clients. Other headhunters are retained and work in high end positions, often starting at the VP level.

Strictly for informational purposes, I can tell you that retained headhunters—sometimes called "search consultants"—often receive one third of the estimated total fee for the candidate up front, one third in 30 days, and the last one third in sixty days or upon presentation of the three qualified candidates required to meet the agreed upon contractual obligation. In many circumstance, the fee will be paid to the search consultant even if no candidate is hired. The specific arrangements of retained searches vary between organization and client, but the same rule always applies to you, the job seeker: Don't ask.

Corporate Recruiters

No discussion of recruiting would be complete without examining corporate recruiters. Those men and women work inside the walls of corporate America, usually as direct employees. Once in a while they're brought in on contract to help with staffing requirements. Corporate recruiters usually report to Human Resources, but the place where the rubber meets the road is the relationship between the hiring manger and the corporate recruiter. For the sake of simplicity, let's say the recruiter usually handles more positions— called requisitions or "reqs"—than a headhunter handles. The real clients of a corporate recruiter are the hiring managers. These managers are usually happy if they have a steady stream of qualified candidates to interview.

Your first point of contact with a company may come as a phone call from a corporate recruiter who wants to set up a phone screen, or perhaps an interview, with the hiring manager. This is good news, so I strongly suggest you avoid the mistake made by too many people:

Do not try to roll over a corporate recruiter and charge right in to see the hiring manager. The corporate recruiter largely determines who the hiring manager will interview.

My advice? Let the corporate recruiter act as your representative and tell the hiring manager how wonderful you are. Be on your best behavior, ask relevant questions, give positive and truthful answers, and use specific performance examples. Make this the best interview of your life, because if you convince the corporate recruiter to pass you on to the hiring manager, you'll probably land an interview.

Make the corporate recruiter look good, and you'll have him on your side. With that endorsement, it's clear sailing for you and the hiring team to go the distance. Of course, you'll be on your own when it comes to showing the organization what you know, what you've done, and how you've achieved success.

Corporate recruiters are a different breed. They may have come from within the ranks of human resources, or perhaps they were hired directly from an agency or some other place. The buzz in recruiter land about agency verses corporate is long, endless, boring, and ultimately unanswerable. Just remind yourself that the standard rules of manners and responsiveness apply to both headhunters and corporate recruiters. Some of these folks are sales oriented, while others are more corporate and procedural minded. They're no better or worse than agency headhunters—they're just a different breed, with different political agendas and, at times, differing types of pressure and priorities.

Bottom line? Consider where they're coming from and don't make their jobs harder. Do all you can to help them support the internal hiring managers, and they will remember you in a positive light. Don't waste their time with endless phone calls. A quick question by e-mail is far better than leaving voice mails and/or playing phone tag. As with outside headhunters, they'll call if, and when, they have something to tell you.

Are recruiters good or bad for your career? That depends on your perspective and current situation. I believe in most cases, they can be a strong asset to your career. There is an adage about three types of customers: good, better, and best. This adage holds true for recruiters as well. Your goal is to help your recruiter be the best he or she can be, regardless of their true motives and capabilities. Getting the most out of recruiters, both internal and external, isn't terribly hard if you remember that all relationships are two-way interchanges. Prepare to give before you expect to take.

Chapter 9

You're Working on Your Resume—Again?

> *"Reason for leaving last position: Pushed aside so the*
> *vice president's girlfriend could steal my job."*
> —Source Unknown

Your Resume

*I*f you type the words "Resume Writing" into Google, your trusty computer will find over 1,410,000 hits. Most of these sites are from so-called experts who want to help you create a perfect resume. Amid all the information, misinformation, and conflict, how do you even know where to start?

I offer you value of a different type. Besides a few personal prejudices for layout or fonts, I will mostly give you a better perspective—an enhanced vantage point from which to consider the resume and its implications. I do this because I'm a gatekeeper; a first line resume-reader who acts as the critical eye. I'm the one who stands in judgment on your obsessive resume writing efforts. I'm the person who actually reads them, ranks them, reviews them with hiring managers (hence to be called HMs), and knows what will work and what will fall short.

Let's begin with the most important characteristic of your resume: the psychological aspect of actually being happy, satisfied, and confident about the document you've created.

Few things are as vexing, mystical, and confounding as your resume. Whether online or in print, this document is both a source of pride and a source of frustration, pain, and insecurity. Preparing your resume is the stuff of which nightmares are made. It can take on a life force of its own if you fail to master it, subdue it, and get the task behind you. Keep messing with it, and you'll have tiny resumes dancing in your dreams, which does nothing good for your sense of wellbeing. I know people who work on their resumes every day. This type of obsessive behavior keeps us from doing the real work that's required to reach our professional goals. Instead of searching for a job, you tell people, "I'm going to spend the day reworking my resume … again."

Let's review a few sample conversations and see if you recognize yourself here:

"Hi, how are you doing?"

"Fine; I was just working on my resume."

"How's the job hunt going?'

"Slow. I think I need to work on my resume."

"Hey, just touching base to see how your job search is progressing. Everything good?"

"Not great; I think I need to work on my resume."

All good questions: all bad answers.

With this in mind, please read these talking points about resumes. After that, we can move on to bigger and better things that *will* happen when you spend time on the real work of finding employment. Please note that endlessly changing this word and moving that comma because you saw another resume you believe was better than yours will make you crazy. Chances are, the resume you saw has no more, or less, impact potential than your resume. The acid test? If you change words and endlessly change them back, then you're deep into the obsessing stage, and you need to put an end to this. Honestly, if it's that bad, you may need an intervention.

There Is No Perfect Resume

Like any document, a resume's worth is based upon the perception of its readers, and you can't expect to impress everyone, no matter how well-crafted it is. When a HM picks up your resume, he'll scan for key words and bits of experience that tell him whether to place it in the "interview" pile or the "no interview" pile.

> Let's start with a simple fact: the perfect resume does not exist. It never did and never will.

This decision is usually based upon how your experience matches the position's requirements. He won't be judging your font, style, or layout. For most hiring managers, the only good resume is the one that makes them want to talk to you.

Lose the Length

I have seen resumes so long, detailed, and over-the-top they look like full feature books. This won't help your cause in the long run, because no HM wants to read a seven pound resume. As mentioned above, HMs seldom read resumes—they scan for particular data, giving the most attention to your first page. Going back too far is of no interest to them. For example, they're much more concerned to see if you opened up a new sales territory in the last job, rather than ten or twelve years ago on page three. Current experience is fresh, represents who you are now, and reflects the current state of the economy.

Resume writer extraordinaire David Roper of the Ascript Group in Marblehead, Massachusetts, recommends keeping your resume to a single page. I tend to agree with him, but I can see having two pages. Beyond that, you are not helping your cause. No one will read page three—and forget about page four. Are you listening? Most recruiters are swamped and overburdened. According to my amazingly talented recruiting buddy, Greg Bennett of the Mergis

Group, the time for static resumes is over. Sell the product that is you in the first few lines, or you'll wish you did.

Further advice from Greg: a resume should change with the job for which you're applying. Keep the bullet points short and use hyperlinks to your blog, appropriate social media sites, and anything else you deem appropriate to support your candidacy. Want to go on endlessly? Do it on LinkedIn. Always keep in mind that the HMs want to know what you've done lately, not during your entire life. What's that you tell me? You're so great that you can't get it all on two pages? You say they'll have questions if you don't squeeze it all in there? Good! Questions are great, because they give you something to discuss on a phone screen or during an interview. Honestly, if you tell them everything, what's left to discuss in the interview? Delete every unnecessary word.

Avoid Fancy

Fancy is a distraction, because content is far more important than format. Monster block type letters with neon lights and your picture on a spring loaded device that pops out when the envelope is opened are not a good thing. If you do that and give the HM a heart attack, it will not work to your favor. Plain and simple rule the day. Deliver a clean resume, with no errant marks or coffee stains. For your font, use a twelve point sans serif text, going to eleven point if necessary, but no smaller. If the HM needs a magnifying glass to read your resume you'll just annoy him, and he'll toss it onto the slush pile. Remember, hiring managers read endless resumes.

Should you bold important things? Perhaps, but not many items. When you bold text, you're telling the HM she's too dumb to know that's important, so you decided to make it big and brash for her. A touch of bold is acceptable, but don't get carried away and make it into a singing and dancing document. I see resumes every day that are so alive they almost frighten me. Simple and readable with reasonable utilization of white space is a good rule of thumb.

Translation: using 1/16 inch margins while cramming every single factoid about you on a page is just plain creepy. Don't do it.

Emphasize Results, Not Responsibilities

When I read your resume, I want to know what you've achieved and the results you have to show for your efforts. I'm not all that interested in your past responsibilities—and the HM will feel the same way, in almost every case.

"Increased sales by 39 percent in NY Metro area." That's a good statement and impresses me. It is short, clear, contains a metric, and seems like quite an accomplishment. When the HM or I meet with you, we'll press a bit and ask how you did it. The statement certainly gets my attention and makes me want to connect with you, which is exactly what you want.

"Full responsibility for sales in NY Metro area," is far less meaningful, because it doesn't tell me anything about what you accomplished. I read it and suspect it's a good thing, but it doesn't strike the chord that will make me reach out and pick up the phone. Lots of people are responsible for very important things, but that doesn't mean they handled any of that responsibility in a way that will be attractive to our organization. Someone was responsible for getting help to Hurricane Katrina victims in New Orleans, but they certainly wouldn't put that on a resume.

"Developed project management tools resulting in cost reduction of 11 percent, which was a savings of almost $211,000." This is good.

"Full responsibility for all aspects of project management on last three major projects." This is not so good.

Avoid Buzz Words

Tell me dear reader, are you a world-class thinker—an out-of-the-box innovator, on message and on target? Highly creative? Are you an accomplished implementer of best-of-breed solutions? Have you analyzed, corrected, and implemented everything you've touched during your career? Have you coached, empowered, and guided others? Have you conceived, directed, implemented, revamped, or upgraded everything in your path?

If so, you're either the best employee on the planet, or you've been reading the resume tips on power words and are suffering from what's commonly known as *buzzworditis*. Okay, that isn't a real disease. I made it up to get my point across.

Dear reader, go easy on the buzz words. Resumes must sound real, not contrived or overly architected by an action/power word writing expert. A few buzz words sprinkled here and there are fine, as long as you demonstrate your accomplishments in clear, definitive terms. Having every other word on the page read like a who's who of power terms and expressions makes me chuckle, but earns you no real advantage. You'll be doing both of us a favor if you present yourself in the best possible light, using clear, concise terms.

Beware of Exaggeration

Come in a bit closer to the page so I can whisper something to you. Just a bit closer now. Ready? Pssst; there are times when people who submit resumes fib a bit. Truth be told, this is almost expected, because we all like to look our best. On the other hand, I suggest you stick to the real story and avoid tall tales. Did you coach Barack Obama from obscurity to an over the top presidential win in 2008 as you stumped the pollsters and delivered this historic win? Great stuff, and if it's all true then add it to the resume. On the other hand, if you simply posted your ideas to his campaign site and noticed he did exactly what you suggested, you might not want to list it as a specific accomplishment. Can you see the difference?

It Is Not Okay to Lie on a Resume.

Sooner or later, those lies will cause problems for you. If you were part of a team that accomplished great things, then say so, but state your specific role and accomplishments. Do not claim a university degree you didn't earn. That's a bad thing to do and will alienate everyone who trusted you.

> Yes, it's acceptable to spin—to present things in the best light, slightly embellish, and add polish to all you've accomplished, but that's the limit. Once you cross the line and begin making untrue statements, grossly exaggerating, or taking credit that's due another, you've become a resume felon.

If you're caught in a lie, do not say you're bipolar, went off your medications, or had a bad father. Do not do ANY of these things. They damage not only you, but also the people who believed in you.

No Functional Resumes

Functional resumes aren't seen as often as they once were, but occasionally someone decides doing one is a great idea. It is *not* a great idea. It's a terrible idea. A functional resume lists your specific experience and skills, rather than giving a chronological list of work experience. Functional resumes make me break out in hives and itch all over, because I can't understand what you accomplished, when you accomplished it, or where you accomplished it. These resumes tend to be vague—and vague is not good in a resume. I won't even take the time to show you what a functional resume looks like, because I don't want this type of dangerous information floating around for anyone to see. Honestly, this is dangerous stuff. If your goal is to give the reader enough information to decide your interview fate, then use a functional resume only if you never wish to be interviewed again.

> Repeat after me: "I will never use a functional resume."

Should you be one of the unlucky folks who already has a functional resume, I implore you to change to a chronological resume as soon as possible. I hate to sound stuffy but in the real world, a chronological resume is the only acceptable format. It should begin with your most recent experience and accomplishments and move back in time from there. This approach is easy to follow and clear to the reader. Furthermore, it's convenient to refer to and discuss during a telephone conversation or interview. Please, I must stop writing about this, because I'm starting to itch.

Have More Than One Resume

How can one do that you ask? You're only one person with one job history. How can you possibly have two different resumes? Let me tell you a story. Back in the day, I was interviewing a candidate brought in to speak about a position that reported to our CEO. They invited me into the interview to lend my opinion about the candidate's background. I remember sitting with him and reviewing his resume as we chatted. I had a good understanding of the position because I helped draft the job description, and I was strong as a business development person in the first place. I felt comfortable doing that interview. At one point in the conversation, I mentioned the position was a combination of several different functions, including business development, account/client management, and search. It was three different functions rolled into one position. (Often, not a good idea.) I really wanted to see how he handled this type of conversation, because if hired, he might be my boss—and I didn't want to work for someone who couldn't teach me some new things.

When I asked if he might highlight some of his experience in the different areas, what came next absolutely floored me. He opened his briefcase, pulled out three different folders, and handed me three distinct resumes. I can still quote him after all these years: "Here's my business development resume, here's my client relations resume, and here's my search resume." I was speechless. I'd never heard of a person with two resumes, let alone three. This fellow had capitalized on his career in ways that accentuated all the good things he'd done in a host of different areas. He then used the resumes to best market his capabilities. We hired him, and he taught me a lot.

If you're a recent grad with a short work history, it won't be easy to prepare multiple resumes, but that's okay. On the other hand, if you're a ten-year-plus veteran with war stories and different accomplishments, I urge you to develop resumes that reflect the position for which you're applying. You should review the resumes you've already developed and tweak them, based upon the position you want. Assuming you stick to the straight story and present yourself in a forthright and honest manner, it's in your best interest to present yourself just this way. The hiring manager should be able to see you in a light that accentuates how your accomplishments relate to the specific position requirements. Are you a project manager who is also a Java Developer? Are you an HR professional who also manages finance and recruiting? Beware of using one resume because you don't want to sell yourself short. The job hunt is not a time to be shy about what you've accomplished.

Attach a Cover Letter

Yes, I did say eight talking points, so consider this extra material a bonus. A cover letter is a good thing to send in conjunction with your resume, and I enjoy reading them. It doesn't take the place of a resume, but it helps you make a high impact statement before I launch into your resume. For that reason, it's worth including a cover letter when you have the opportunity.

For example, saying in the cover letter that you just left ABC company after building the professional services group from $700,000 to $14,000,000 in four years will certainly get my attention—and that's exactly what you want. Remember: cover letters should provide the "why" and the "wow" in short form to whet the reader's appetite for your resume.

Cover letters should meet three important criteria:

1. The cover letter should touch upon a few details of your background that relate to the position for which you're applying. Keep it short and to the point. For example, if you're applying for a position as an architect, you might note that you have strong real-world experience designing the types of buildings for which your prospective employer is well known. Feel free to drop the names of recent projects I might've heard of. Listing Fenway Park as an edifice you designed would get the wrong type of attention, so consider the laws of relevancy

Newer and more familiar always trump more distant time-lines and obscure credits.

2. The cover letter should contain a few sentences, perhaps two or three short bullet points, and a closing sentence thanking the reader for considering the resume. If you make the cover letter the size of a book, you'll destroy the advantage of having a cover letter in the first place.

3 The cover letter should be personalized to the individual who'll receive it. This is, after all, a letter. It should be simple, polite, and easy to read. The letter is the first and only chance you'll have to open with a favorable impression, and I suggest you use that opportunity wisely.

If you can use this information to create a resume that's easy to read, clear, and of reasonable length, you'll be doing everyone, yourself included, a huge favor. Despite other things you might have seen or read, confusion and obfuscation on a resume will not put you on the road to meaningful and multiple interviews.

Chapter 10

Got References?

*"He is just great. Really the best there is,
and I have no time for these things."*
—Opening line from
a reference I did years ago

A strong reference is second only to a strong interview in advancing your job quest. The words of a trusted reference will add credence to your story and reinforce your qualifications and skills. I assure you they often help an on-the-fence hiring manager decide between you and another leading candidate. This alone is a great reason to do the reference thing properly.

References are consultative in nature; a quiet, delicate conversation between two people. The person who gives you a reference should know you and your capabilities well. His or her words add credibility to your resume. Hiring managers who are smart enough to understand the importance of the reference use it as a tool to confirm what they already suspect, and to obtain further information in areas that require illumination and clarity. I have seen number two candidates move up to number one spots because of quality references. I've seen candidates get an offer as a result of strong conversations with references who understand the importance of selling their strengths, as opposed to just answering questions like a dunce. A strong reference will be a confirming conversation. The reference check should be a highly targeted exchange that will confirm the credibility of the story you worked so hard so communicate.

Let's consider ten insights into this underrated and misunderstood part of the hiring process.

No One Does References Checks These Days
This is incorrect.

Only clueless people avoid doing reference checks or leave the task for someone else. Sadly, these folks don't understand that references provide the information they need to influence and support hiring decisions.

Even worse is the person who uses a reference only to gain bits of information, such as dates of employment. Here's an example:

"Hello, can you please tell me Bill's start date? Um, my form says he started two days before that. Can you please tell me Bill's end date? Oh, his end date was actually six days before what I have on my form. Can you please confirm Bill's salary? Oh, he must have forgotten about that 2 percent raise. Okay, thank you so much. Have a nice day."

What could be more absurd than the above conversation? When a hiring manager calls for a reference on a possible hire, the person to whom he speaks is filling a critical role. The manager should consider that reference a trusted member of the team. Please don't be lulled into a false sense of complacency, no matter how well the interview process has proceeded. Your references are very important.

You Can't Say Anything Bad in a Reference
This thinking makes me crazy. As a quick aside, I once had a reference shout at me over the phone! "He's a moron. If you want

to hire a moron, he's your guy." Then he slammed the phone down. Do you think we hired that candidate?

The above story is indeed rare, but if you think an HM is going to let your reference person ramble on and on about how you're the best thing since sliced bread, then you're sadly mistaken. A good HM will ask probing questions and consider reference responses carefully. If your reference handles the call correctly, she'll be a strong force to help the HM understand your background, capabilities, and achievements

If done well, this conversation will not only strengthen the HM's understanding of your abilities but will also shed light into areas that might require more development. Please be advised this isn't a bad thing. The reference's objective is not to make the HM believe you are devoid of any faults. The HM doesn't expect you to be perfect. In fact, if your reference isn't honest about your flaws, she may lose credibility and do little to advance your case. A reference who presents you as perfect isn't doing you a favor.

Prep Your References

Be sure your reference is on board with your interview and understands the position for which you hope to receive an offer. The reference can't support your candidacy if she's in the dark. At a bare minimum, she needs to know a good deal about the nature of the position, the organization, the requirements for success, and if possible, a bit about the HM. She also needs to know what should be emphasized and fleshed out during the reference conversation.

Plan the Call

There's nothing worse than a hiring manager who calls a reference out of the blue, during off hours. The resulting conversation is bound to be awkward and choppy—not how you want it to go. Just as you set up your own interview with a time and place, the reference needs to be set up this way as well. Fortunately, that isn't hard to do. Work as the person in the middle to make this happen, and then send a confirming e-mail to both parties. This will save the HM and the reference valuable time in avoiding phone tag.

More importantly, it saves you from the worst thing that can happen in a reference call: one party telling the other he's on the run, but can take five minutes to talk. Shortchanging yourself this way will compromise your job quest instead of showing the HM your true value.

A Good Reference Is a Money Call

If you're being considered for a position that has reached the reference stage, it means the HM is serious. As with most positions, the HM has a range of latitude for your starting compensation. A strong reference can influence your starting salary in a positive way.

Emphasize Value, Results, and Track Record

Just as you should be honest during your interviews, the reference should be forthcoming about your background. Once again, she should provide validation and an accurate reflection of your capabilities, presented in their best possible light. The reference should speak of your value to the organization, the results you achieved, and your track record for success. If handled this way, your reference will have done the job, and you'll be giving the HM good reason to see you as a strong addition to their team.

Keep in Touch

We live in a society where we reach out when we need something, but after that we tend to disappear until next time we're in need. Try to stay in touch with your references, whether you need them or not. They are a vital part of your network. References are people just like you, and none of us wants to be used.

>>>

Keep in touch with your references. No one wants to feel she hears from you only when you need something.

///

I also suggest you avoid the biggest blunder of all—not following up with your reference after the results are in. It matters little if you get the job or not. What matters is that you communicate the results as soon as they're in and thank the reference for her time and assistance. Don't make your job-search partners find out what happened through the grapevine.

Give Managers As References

Using peers and even subordinates as references is in vogue these days, because we live in a society where many people believe everything we do or say is okay. This is absurd on all levels. I strongly suggest you give the names of those persons within the organization to whom you reported. They will have the most clout and credibility with the HM who's looking at you as a candidate. They can achieve a peer-to-peer connection with the HM, creating a sense of confidence and trust. Do you have no one to whom you were a direct report? Go to a dotted line report as a next step. If not, try to find any senior level person who knows you well enough to speak of your background and accomplishments, even if there was no direct reporting relationship. Go to a peer next, if that's the best you can do, but understand the credibility factor may be compromised. Beyond that, you have a problem because many HMs don't view subordinates as viable references.

Use Customers As References

Are you a salesperson seeking a similar position? If so, it's a terrific idea to list a few customer references. The HM's primary question will be simple: "I know you could have purchased this salami from many different people. Why did you buy it from him/

her?" This is a powerful question, and if answered correctly, can change the course of events in your life. If that reference sells you to the HM, you may be on your way to bigger and better things.

Choose the Right References

If you have the luxury of possessing a host of great references, use the ones who will sell you to the HM. Choose people who have a bit of excitement in their voices—the ones who will crackle when they speak of you. They don't need to sound like an infomercial for a new juicer, but they should have genuine interest and excitement about you and your career. Remember, you want the HM to hang up the phone with a real sense of believing you're the person for the job. This is far more likely to happen if the reference is alive on the phone, as opposed to someone who passively answers questions.

A last thought on references. How many references should you give the HM? That number is up to you. Some people dole them out in ones and twos like they were golden eggs, saying, "If you have trouble reaching those people, I'll give you another one." Perhaps it's an issue of style, but that isn't how I like to play the game. My aggressive nature drives me to give five references to anyone who requests them. If I could manage to contact everyone, I'd give out 20 or so and tell the client they have permission to speak with everyone who's ever known me, going as far back as they like. I feel this way because I've worked hard for a long time, and I'm proud of my accomplishments. I can't imagine not being delighted to have a potential client call around to check me out. Since great references are truly riches to the interviewee, can having the occasional embarrassment of riches be such a bad thing?

I urge you to think long and hard about how you handle, manage, and prep your references. Those contacts can make a significant difference in how things turn out when you're a serious candidate for a position. Please consider all I've said and take references seriously. More than that, I suggest you consider references your "last interview." A reference check is the interview you do not attend. Your background, temperament, accomplishments, motivation, and potential fit for a position are carefully examined and evaluated. Your references are, in a sense, character witnesses. This level of examination should be taken seriously, because once you reach the reference stage, you're so close. I urge you to rethink your ideas on references.

Chapter 11
The Interview: Insights and Essential Thinking

"Would it be a problem if I'm angry most of the time?"
—Actual question from a job interview gone bad.

The Interview

You receive a call from either a hiring manager (HM) or someone in Human Resources asking you to come in for an interview. The time and place are established, and you're on the way to achieving greatness.

At this point, a wide range of conflicting emotions may flood your psyche. You may experience fear, mingled with excitement. You may feel a sense of dread and unease. Some people suffer acute anxiety that seeps into everything they do. This is normal.

> Few things cause more stress in life then a job interview looming on the horizon.

The HM is going to judge you, assesses your true abilities in comparison to other candidates, and rank you. This can be frightening; no one likes being judged.

In anticipation of the interview, we relive past events and imagine future possibilities. We try to bury the demons and insecurities that haunt us, but though they're well-disguised, we carry wounds and self-doubt with us like a second skin. Few of us have the thick skin we pretend to possess—myself included.

Where do we go from here? The interview creeps closer. We do more research. We create imaginary questions and answers. The red tie or the striped one comes to mind each time we open our closet. Red pumps, or black? (Men should not wear red pumps. Ever.) The future is in our hands, and we can't mess up.

I knew a candidate who became so nervous he actually got sick before each interview. As an aside, the great Bill Russell of the Boston Celtics had the same problem before game time, but he certainly was a superstar player. Honestly, the angst we suffer is so unnecessary. Next to resume advice, more has been written about interviewing than any other job hunting skill. Much of the information sounds reasonable, while other comments are just plain weird.

I've read that "aping" the interviewer creates a subliminal bond between the two of you—a connection that will give you an advantage. Perhaps this is the psychological edge we all seek. So you go into the interview prepared to copy the interviewer's body language. He leans back in the chair; you lean back in your chair. He thinks pensively, holding his left index finger to his temple; you do likewise. He scratches his chin, and you scratch yours. If he has a stroke and falls on the floor, do you fall beside him? Dear reader, I ask you never to ape the interviewer. If you can manage this I will be one happy writer, because I suspect that aping is for, well … apes.

Aside from the tidbit above, let's consider eight talking points relating to the interview from my side of the desk—the side where thumbs up or thumbs down determines the fate of your candidacy. I hope this overview of interviewing will help you discover a better way to approach and navigate your interview. My goal is to have a heart-to-heart talk with you; to coach you and shed light on a different way to see and approach the interview. I wish to reduce fear, angst, and unrealistic expectations.

Reframe Your Mindset About the Interview

Do not look at the interview as an interview. Think of it as a conversation. Failing to do this will make you edgy, which does nothing to help your performance. Picture yourself sitting on one side of the desk and the interviewer on the other, having a conversation about possibilities.

During the last dozen years I've been interviewed by many clients as I sold my recruiting and consulting services. I've done every type of interview in the book: informational interviews, fact gathering interviews, group interviews, presentation interviews, and others that were just exploratory in nature. They're all the same on some level. Interviews are a dialogue between two people. They give you an opportunity to explore possibilities and show what you're capable of doing.

Approaching the interview as a conversation will make you feel more comfortable and in control. Once you've taken a seat in the room, I suggest you inhale, exhale, and center yourself. I urge you to see the interviewer across the table from you as just another person—someone who has his own good days and bad days, just like you.

Try to take some joy in the time you spend together. With the goal of having an intelligent and engaging conversation, follow in any direction the interviewer wishes to travel. On the other hand, you should also be comfortable enough to move the subject matter in another direction if you believe doing so will play to your strengths or the interviewer's requirements.

Remember, this is a two-way conversation, and the interviewer needs to hear your take on all of it: your experience, insights, and ideas for new and creative approaches. Present your thoughts in a dynamic, give-and-take style, and you'll be doing your part to make the interview a success.

Try To Relax

Nothing makes me more nervous than a candidate who's hyperventilating during the interview. Perceiving that person as a wreck interferes with my ability to have the nice conversation I hope to enjoy with every candidate. Most interviewers do want candidates to be comfortable and enjoy the experience. The last thing in the world I want is to spend an hour talking with a candidate who's humming with anxiety. I find it draining and spend the rest of the day in a state of exhaustion. Again, this isn't major surgery; no one is cutting you open. It's just a conversation. If you're on the verge of falling apart, the interviewer will sense it, and this will not help you.

Looking for a way to relax a bit? I suggest you view the interview as a two-way street. They're interviewing you, and you're also interviewing them. You might be looking for a position, but you need the right position—not the first one that comes along. You should be seeking the best possible offer, and not just from the standpoint of compensation.

Trading money for misery is seldom a good deal. Look around and think things over. Do you like them? Are you comfortable during the interview process? How did they make you feel while you were there? Were you treated as a welcome guest or as an annoyance in their busy day? Do you have a clear idea about what you'd be doing there each day? Is it a miserable commute? Why is the job open? If seven people have gone through that job during the last three years and they all failed, is taking that job a good idea? (I think not. What are you, Superman?)

Yes, the interviewers are judging you, but go into the interview with confidence, because you're also judging them. Do you have an idea how many people interview, receive offers, and turn those offers down every day? Endless numbers. Rejection happens from both sides, so never forget that each interview is a two-way street.

Looking for another reason to relax? Having been on the inside, I assure you the interview matters far less than you might think, for a host of reasons. Sadly, you won't necessarily get a job just because you do a great interview. Furthermore, you may not land the job even if you're the best candidate. A great deal of this is directly related to the person who conducts the interview, and these folks can be broken down into three categories:

1. Those who know exactly what they're looking for.
2. Those who will know what they're looking for once they've seen it.
3. Those who still don't know what they're looking for, even after they've seen it (and probably never will.)

All too often, the hiring team across the interview table isn't exactly sure what they want. This can sometimes work in your favor if you can tell them what they want and show them you *are* that person. With that in mind, answer questions effectively and clearly. Put them at ease by using an evocative, quick, and on-point story or example, if possible. Remember to smile. Ask a few of your own questions (preferably open ended as opposed to closed), and try to coax a genuine laugh from the person doing the interview, if that's a strength of yours. If you can manage this, you'll have had a great interview, and the hiring manager will remember you in a positive way. And that's the best you can hope for most of the time.

Be Realistic

Few things offer more hope and less chance of success than a well-orchestrated interview. This is a sad reality of the hiring process. Wonder why? It's the nature of the beast, and here are a few examples:

- Many candidates will be interviewed.
- The hiring team often makes modifications in the position requirements based upon organizational changes and/or new departmental objectives. (This may happen after you've been interviewed.)

- The position might be frozen, eliminated, or filled by an internal candidate.
- The company or department may reorganize and place the position on hold.

The possibilities are almost endless.

Don't be unrealistic about the position or the process and expect to be hired simply because your qualifications match their specifications. This kind of thinking is a dangerous approach.

Matching your qualifications with a position's specifications works well when choosing antifreeze for your car by matching the driving condition specs on the bottle to your vehicle and geographic location. It doesn't work so well with human, political, or business elements—especially in the world of employment.

After the interview, try to feel happy with the effort you made. Never beat yourself up after an interview. Send a thank you to all of those concerned and follow up where appropriate, but don't make the interviewer crazy with calls and e-mails, because that will not help your cause.

Please be advised that your followup e-mail to thank them for the time spent should be short and to the point. Just say thank you. This isn't the time to go on endlessly and try to sell them on your qualifications one more time. This isn't the time to tell them once again why you're perfect for the position. The time to make that point has passed. Just a nice, short thank you is a perfect way to reach out and conclude the process.

I Am Perfect For the Job

I hear these words all the time: "I'm perfect for the job." It makes me crazy, and furthermore it does nothing to help you gain credibility. No one is perfect for a job. Life just doesn't work that way, and conveying that statement to the HM will not help your case. In fact, it shows poor business judgment at exactly the moment when you need to exhibit superior business skills. A company is considering you for a job because they have an ongoing problem and are willing to spend money to fund this position and solve their issues. Business problems are thorny, complex, political, and often moving targets. Saying you're perfect tells the HM you underestimate the problem, making you sound like an amateur. That is not a good thing.

I assure you I'm not perfect for my job and probably never will be. Last time I checked, I was human. I struggle for mastery, but I'll never achieve it. Let me remind you, the interviewer isn't perfect either—not even close.

Sometimes I see the opposite problem. HMs knock at my door and tell me they just met the perfect person for the job. That's their version of being equally unrealistic. When we discuss the candidate in detail, we each begin to see the shortcomings and flaws we hoped to avoid, because we want the laborious, flawed, and unscientific process of hiring to go away. As you can see, finding a perfect candidate isn't the answer from this side of the table either.

Allow me to shed light on the hiring process from the other side of the desk. Do you hate looking for a job? I assure you almost everyone feels the same way.

What about the person who's responsible for hiring? Can you see it from that angle—from the pain of having to make the right hire? Most HMs hate their part in this process: the procedures, the politics, the administrative work, and all the hoops present countless nightmares. Just getting permission to hire someone can mean a weak of distress. Can you understand why so few managers see hiring as part of their job? They're wrong, of course, because hiring, just like firing, is a mission critical part of management.

One of the worst elements of an employee resignation is the HM's realization that she must now replace this person. Yet again, she will have to go through the miserable hiring process.

Selecting the right employee from a small group of strangers never includes a crystal ball or safety net. Results are not guaranteed, and business du jour is painfully disrupted during the hiring process.

Here's another, more personal, reason to avoid thinking you're perfect for a job. If you don't get the job in a world where you believed you were the perfect match, you feel victimized. That's the last idea you want creeping into your head. "I was absolutely perfect for that job, but I didn't get it." You believe you've been dealt a terrible injustice, but in reality you had unrealistic expectations.

I suggest a different approach. If you go in seeing yourself as a great candidate for the job, you'll be far better off. Speak to your accomplishments and skills. For example, if I'm interviewing you for an IT position, talk about the things you've done and your success in the IT areas related to the position you want. Show me you understand the scope of possibilities that exist in this position. Tell me a story of success—of hardship and triumph, thanks to your persistence in overcoming all odds to create a winning solution. Make me envision you in the position we're discussing. If you can do this, you've taken your first step toward being a viable candidate. Remember this: never leave an interview wishing you'd told the HM this or that. I would rather say something I regretted than omit something I now consider to be of importance.

Timing Is Everything

All your life you've heard that timing is everything. Getting hired is no exception to that rule. Tell me—if you were going to fly on a plane, would you buy a parachute? Probably not. What about if the doors blew off and you were about to fall through the open door of that plane at 50,000 feet? Would you buy a parachute then? I suspect you would, and that's an example of timing in action.

I tell you this because I've seen excellent candidates not get a job they hoped for, and a few weeks later the need for that position skyrockets. The HMs feel terror and quickly hire someone because they fear they can't survive without filling the position. Was the person hired over you a better candidate? Probably not. But once again, hiring isn't even close to being an exact science. I can't tell you how many times I've been stunned to see a candidate chosen for a position over other people who were a far better fit. On the other hand, I can't tell you how many times I've seen fabulous candidates who are the first to interview get passed over so the hiring team can interview other candidates. I can understand wanting to see other candidates. My big gripe here is that so many members of the hiring team have a built-in prejudice: a belief that you should never hire the first candidate you interview. I assure you, from a statistical standpoint the first candidate interviewed has the same probability of being the right candidate as the third or the fifth. Unfortunately, hiring teams don't always have a grasp of statistics.

Once you begin the interviewing game, the issue of timing is something you must accept. Don't let an accident of timing destroy your positive attitude, and don't read too much into it. The universe isn't working against you. Some things are random. Your new mantra: "I will find a better position, but they will not find a better employee." Believe it. Say it aloud and move on.

The Interviewer Didn't Like Me

Let's say it right here and be done with it: the balance of power in an interview is as far out of whack as it can possibly be. The interviewer has all of the power and the candidate has none. Like it or not, that's the name of that game, and there's little you can do to change that scenario. If the interviewer doesn't like how you knotted your tie or the way you looked at him; if he feels threatened in any way, he can pass on you. End of story. Furthermore, there's little you can do to make things turn out differently. The brutal reality of this unequal distribution of power is simple. We can rest assured no one is going to hire a person with whom they feel threatened, uncomfortable, or flat out dislike.

Strangely enough, this scenario has an upside. Believe me, you don't want to work with someone who doesn't like you. It may seem better in the short run to have that job, but we can't engage in short-term thinking. Ultimately, working under someone who dislikes you won't come to any good. Sooner rather than later, you'll be searching for another position, wondering why you were displaced. You don't need this type of stress to make you feel like one of life's employment victims. Having a hiring manager reject you up front because you don't have, as the saying goes, "the right DNA" can be a blessing in disguise.

> During my career I've seen employees whose fondest wish was to kill each other.

That isn't what you want for your work life. The objective, once again, is to get the right job—not just any job. If the good chemistry isn't there, then let it go. Consider yourself fortunate. If you know in your heart you don't want to work for a company; if you feel uncomfortable with the HM or during your tour of the office, then taking the job is a dangerous business.

The Job Is Mine To Lose: I will ace the interview

Let me be blunt. No, and no again. This is dangerous thinking and first cousin to the myth "I am perfect for the position." I can assure you this attitude won't help you and does nothing for your mental wellbeing. You have no idea about the competition, which may include internal as well as external candidates. How can you believe the job is yours to lose if you don't even know your competition or the politics of the organization? Perhaps an internal person has been groomed for this role for years, but the company requires the HM to interview three different candidates. What if your interview is a formality, with the results already decided, and you never had a chance at the job for which you felt perfect.

Secondly, if you employ intellectual honestly and real business savvy, your expectation of acing the interview is unrealistic. You probably have no insight whatsoever regarding the HM's decision criteria. Your version of "acing the interview" and the HM's version of "acing the interview" may be two distinctly different things. And only one version counts.

Going into an interview with this kind of expectation is a recipe for disaster—and why make a challenging endeavor even more difficult? A word of caution about people who try to help you along the way. Family and friends can be wonderful, but beware those who tell you there's no one on the planet better than you for that job. Such comments plant seeds for a type of pressure that isn't helpful to you. Thank them for their support, but don't embrace the message. Instead, embrace the mission.

> Your goal is to be invited back so you can move to the next step in the process and receive an offer. Forget about acing the interview. Do your best to connect and demonstrate value.

Assume a Consultative Approach

A consultant is someone who's brought in to help an organization by supporting them with experience and/or expertise not available in house. (Please don't confuse a consultant with a contract worker who, though highly skilled, is essentially another pair of hands that allow the organization to do more work without creating a new full time position.) Consultants, when interviewing, tend to focus more on solving problems than on the long-term issues associated with employment. Most often, they are there to fix a problem and move on.

Approaching a job interview like a consultant has certain advantages. For openers, it allows the people interviewing you to see how your thought process and creativity may help take away their pain. This approach shows you as the problem solver they're hoping to find. You stand out from the rest of the pack, because most people see interviewing as a question and answer session— which isn't necessarily a good thing. Yes, to a degree, the HM asks questions and you answer those questions, but that can be a one-dimensional experience. Even great answers to a HM's questions won't necessarily cause the interviewer to have the leap of faith, the emotional high, and the confidence to put you on the short list of candidates who will move to the next level. Taking a consultative point of view can help put you ahead of the pack, because it's an action-oriented approach and a more aggressive way to interview. This approach leaves a stronger impression and creates excitement in the mind of the HM.

Consider this: if you're interviewing for a full-time position, it means there's a problem and someone within the organization believes that problem is serious enough to hire a full-time person to fix or manage it. For example, if you're being interviewed for a Systems Analyst position, they obviously need more help than they can get from their current team of System Analysts. That's why they committed a budget for the position—they need the right person to solve that problem. Wouldn't it be great if the people interviewing you saw you as that potential problem solver? Can you see how that's exactly what you want to happen? You want to be perceived as the answer to their problem. Their post interview team debriefing should sound like this: "If we hire Frank, we can hand all of this over to him, and we won't have to worry about it." That's exactly what you want them to say about you after you walk out of the building. They want to say it as well, because I assure you they wish to make this problem go away as quickly as possible.

The consultative approach is a gentle swing away from the standard question-and-answer routine. The consultative approach allows you, at some point in the conversation, to take control and say magic words like these: "Listen, I have an idea. Let me tell you what I'd do if it was my problem right now." Saying that, or any variation of the statement, is one of the most powerful tools you can employ in an interview. It sets you apart from the rest, because after receiving enough information to comment intelligently, you do so and impress your hosts with not only strategic thinking, tactical thinking as well. This takes guts, but I see it as worth the risk if you want to stand out.

Let's take an example and play it out with an employer. Let's assume the problem is prolonged hold times for technical support calls, leading customers to complain or hang up. The firm has no budget for new support agents, nor do they want to raise the price of the product to cover that added expense. Here's what you might say, "I would consider selling a priority customer support package that guarantees hold times of no more than two minutes, plus 24-hour call backs on unresolved issues. This represents real value to your customer. The revenue generated by selling these priority support packages will cover the additional employees required. These employees can be cross trained for up-selling new software releases on the products they support. They can also make appointments for the sales staff to demo new products to existing customers. I initiated something like this for my previous employer, and it worked out well. Does that sound reasonable to you?"

Can you feel the power in this approach? Can you see the impact? A free solution to the person doing the interviewing, opposed to just another Q and A. Do you see how this sets you apart?

In the end, it's important to understand that every interview is a crapshoot. It might turn into something, and it might not. Truth be told, even an interview that results in nothing further isn't a failure. With each interview you get out in front of people, you speak, listen, think, and look at the angles.

If you don't get the job, that's yesterday's news. Life goes on. Other jobs await you, so go back to the search and just keep trying.

If it happens to turn out well, that's a wonderful thing. If not, that outcome has to be okay with you as well. Someone once said the only real failure is failure to try. That sentiment clearly fits the realities of the interviewing experience.

Chapter 12
Go with Your Strengths

"Whatever you are by nature, keep to it; never desert your line of talent. Be what nature intended you for, and you will succeed."
—Sidney Smith

The fact that you're reading this manuscript means you're almost certainly looking for something. Perhaps you're hoping for an insight, a sudden brainstorm, or a key idea to help you spin away from entrenched thinking and see your world with fresh eyes. You may be looking for ideas with substance and depth that will lead you out of the difficulty and turmoil of these unpleasant times. If that's your quest, you aren't alone.

Unfortunately, providing these answers is no easy task, because on some level we're all rooting around in the dark, clutching survival knives, and trying to figure out what happened. Fortunately, I can see light at the end of the tunnel.

Everyone reading this text knows that when you lose a job, you look for another. That's how we've been trained. Not only do we look for another job, we nearly always look for the *same* job. Part of human nature is to seek out the comfortable and the familiar. But what happens when that quest no longer works for us—when the jobs we feel good about are no longer available? What happens when the familiar tools we once depended upon have crumbled?

Many of us have struggled to find employment in our own industries, going with our best contacts and practices cultivated over a long period of time. Far too often, the pool of candidates for a given position clearly overwhelms the number of available jobs. That's when you know it's time to consider a different approach, with new options on the table. Here's the first question I often hear: "How can I build a bridge from the known to the unknown?"

What Are Your Real Strengths?

As you begin considering new approaches, the first step is to evaluate what your job search toolbox already contains. I'm willing to bet you have skills, talents, and positive attributes you've never recognized. Instead, you may be focusing on the negatives.

Perhaps you're involved in a personal make-over program of some kind, trying to shore up weak areas of your professional life. You're working to change your wardrobe, re-do your resume (again), find a better hairstyle, hone your interviewing skills, and possibly upgrade your social networking skills and awareness.

There's nothing wrong with self-improvement, but sometimes we work so hard on the negatives that we neglect to appreciate our assets. Doing this is a mistake of epic proportions, because undervaluing our unique strengths instead of capitalizing on them won't help us in the long run. We need to take stock of everything we do well and feel good about. These attributes are the key to future possibilities and new opportunities that will get our lives back on track.

Let me give you an example of why this concept is so important. If you compete for a position that plays to your strengths, you may be seen as one of the top three or four contenders in the race. If you compete for positions that play to your weaknesses, you may not even make the first cut. Half a dozen other candidates who are stronger in these areas will be ahead of you.

> Playing to your strengths is essential when you're competing for the opportunities you decide to pursue.

I've been around for a long time, working for many organizations, in different vertical marketplaces, on teams with new and varied assignments. Over the years, I've learned to identify my strong and weak points. By now, I'm comfortable with who I am, where I can contribute, and where I just get in the way of progress.

My strengths lie in the people end of business life. I have a special talent for forming relationships, establishing trust, and helping those who depend upon me to find solutions to their difficulties. I can calm clients who feel they've been ignored, and I can solve lingering problems. I'm able to influence those around me to move in a given direction through careful persuasion, and I have the ability to show them why my ideas are not only good for the organization, but for them a well. These are specific and valuable strengths.

I can use these talents and skills in business development, sales, or client management. I'm perfect in the world of professional services and in helping to manage deliverables, because I know how to make things happen. I can open clogged and broken lines of communication among those who make war in the workplace and provide solutions that satisfy a wide range of needs. I'm a good listener, and I also know when the time has arrived to pull the trigger on a given plan. I'm almost an artist in my ability to build consensus and create a situation where everyone comes out a winner, because I know how to make the elephant dance. I can even do a bit of writing or speaking if necessary.

Those are my primary strengths, and I play to them when I seek out opportunities. I don't have to specifically be a recruiter if there's no need for recruiters, but I still have to play on the basic strengths that make me an excellent recruiter. Fortunately, these positive attributes are perfect for a host of different employment areas. As I see it, we will always need those strengths in situations where people disagree, have their own agendas, and would rather be right on a personal level than do what's best for the organization.

My weaknesses? The list is long, but let's begin with numbers and math skills. These words are being written by a person who can't figure ten percent of 100 without a calculator. This is a terrible weakness on my part because numbers are the language of business. I could endlessly struggle to get better at this, but why bother? The best I'll ever become is a person who can barely make numbers work. All I can hope to do is shore up this weakness by compensating and surrounding myself with people who are strong in the areas in which I am weak. For example, if I need projections on numbers relating to plans I've developed, I try to do the math myself, and then run those numbers past someone who has a talent for math. I don't make myself crazy trying to be good at something I find so difficult, yet I still manage to complete my work.

Other weaknesses? Using hand tools, climbing on a roof to hammer a nail, and doing other things that require physical dexterity and a good eye for detail. Armed with this information, I won't play to my weaknesses when looking for another job. I will not become a project manager in the construction industry, because I won't be successful in the long run. I won't try to be an accountant, a carpenter, or a physicist. Even if I managed to enter one of these fields, I'd never be the superstar I believe we all have the capacity to become.

Here's an example: My friend Rob was in sales, but he's also an athlete who loves people and coaches his kid's soccer team. No sales jobs? Rob turned his career around and became a massage therapist. He sells his own services at corporate events and enjoys coaching his clients on how to remain healthy through light weight work and daily stretching. This was a brilliant transition for someone who played to his strengths. (Rob can't add numbers either.)

What about you? Do you know your strengths and weaknesses? We're all good at some things and not so great at others. If you use your strengths to move you forward in the right areas and consider positions that call for these strengths, you'll do far better than if you try shoring up your weaknesses in an effort to compensate.

Do you want to get bold and creative in your job search? Do you want to use this opportunity to break free of the chains that held you in a given position for the last twenty years? Are you thinking of reaching out to different industries and new marketplaces? Play to your strengths.

Chapter 13
Innovate for Professional Survival

Don't give me best practices; they are yesterday's news.
Give me emerging practices. They are tomorrow's news.

—Unknown

Innovate, Yes. Best Practices ... Possibly Not

Job Hunting? I suggest you begin your quest not just by looking for a job, but by carefully deconstructing why you're seeking a job in the first place—and how. Use some type of a metric to see what's working for you and what isn't. For example, what gets you leads and what does not? What gets you interviews and what does not? This, and only this, allows you to know which methods to abandon, which ones to modify, and what you should keep doing because it's getting results.

Let me tell you a story. I had my car washed last month and the man who was drying it handed me a resume and told me he was a recent graduate with a degree in mechanical engineering. I found this tactic brilliant. I read the resume, then emailed him the names of several people he could contact for further help. I also gave him a few links to read that pertained to getting your first job. He sent me an email last week saying he landed a job and asked if I'd connect with him on LinkedIn. Now he has a job, and I have another connection. Did my e-mail referrals help? I don't know, but that doesn't matter, because his creative approach paid off. A lot of cars came though there on a nice Sunday morning, exposing him to a wide variety of people who could offer connections, tips, and encouraging words.

Do I suggest you find work at a car wash to get creative about landing a job? Not necessarily, but on the other hand, I wouldn't look you in the eye and tell you it's bad idea. In reality, the more important question is: if you were already working at the car wash, would you have been innovative enough to hand out YOUR resume? I strongly advise you to reach out to the new and the different, as opposed to just sending a resume to an email address or filling out forms online.

I have nothing against resumes, but snail mailing resumes is an ancient practice. Doing it on the Internet is far more contemporary, but on many levels, it's the same thing, minus a postage stamp. I believe all of us need to reconsider the tried and true methods of job hunting and think about innovation.

Why reinvent the wheel, you ask?

Because at times the wheel isn't exactly rolling along. Perhaps you've already been cruising the Internet, conducting research, sending out resumes, and networking—maybe for a year or longer. This seems reasonable, but are you are getting results? If your answer is, "No, I'm not getting *good* results," then consider changing tactics. What are the options?

I'm glad you asked, because new options are something you can create. Has the marketplace for jobs changed in ways that are so definitive, disruptive, and broken that even the best practices no longer work? I hope not, because then we all have to return to square one and redesign everything we hold dear.

Best practices are accepted methods that have worked historically. Depending upon them as the only answer presents a clear and present danger.

Let me tell you a little secret about best practices: They're built upon the past instead of designed for the future.

Perhaps we should grab these tried and true methods by the scruff of the neck and shake them silly to see if they hold up to the rigors of today's new and complex problems. So where do you go from here?

- Will your answer lie in personal branding and multiple consulting assignments that result in several income sources?
- Could you work within small groups to create jobs, based upon solving specific and measurable problems?
- Is your answer to utilize social media, reaching out to every person who might be able to help with a quick introduction?
- Is the answer to develop a blog with an embedded video that highlights your past accomplishments and your abilities?
- Will you search for a position in a different or related field and develop new talents?
- Will you stand in the subway handing out cards offering $500 for any lead that turns into a job offer?

How far will you go with this type of innovative activity depends upon your comfort level, but trying everything that has a reasonable chance of achieving results is a fine place to start. If you begin seeing results, move forward and increase the level of activity. If one approach fails, you change tactics.

Innovation gives you freedom to experiment, with no track record of real success—and no track record of failure either; just possibilities based upon your creativity. Can you see the advantage here?

I believe the sooner we get rid of those sacred cows known as *best practices* that no longer deliver results, the better off we'll be.

The sooner we trade in accepted dogma for contrarian thinking, the sooner we'll see enhanced results. The sooner we question all we do by measuring its effectiveness, the faster we can innovate. The faster we innovate, the greater the rewards. Can you taste the intense flavor of that idea? Can you imagine the possibilities? Innovation versus best practices? The call is yours, but I urge you to examine, read, and explore. We need as much information as possible to make good decisions, and the information we have in our heads isn't enough. What we know today is at best, only good enough for today. We must plan for tomorrow because that is where our focus needs be.

Are best practices the enemy? Of course not. They led to some of the finest things we do. But we need to understand that best practices should be written in pencil instead of ink. They need to coexist with the many faces of innovation as their roommates. They must be held in balance; each vying for the opportunity to prove itself once again as the best solution. They need to be challenged every day for effectiveness.

To quote Alf Rehn: "Everything works some of the time and nothing works all of the time."

I suggest we all begin seeking out and inventing trends and solutions that will succeed tomorrow, because if you take a quick glance at your watch, you'll see that today is on its way out at breakneck speed. I suggest we prepare for tomorrow by innovating for success.

Chapter 14
Who's Managing YOUR Career?

"The biggest mistake you can make is to believe that you are working for somebody else. Job security is gone. The driving force of a career must come from the individual. Remember: Jobs are owned by the company. You own your career!

—*Earl Nightingale*

Managing Things

*A*re you employed? If so, that's great, but like it or not, you're still at risk. In the professional world, we're all at risk. Please accept that as an uncomfortable fact of life in the workplace and the world at large. We'd all like to believe our jobs are safe as long as we want to work, but that belief doesn't match reality. Organizations are constantly looking for ways to save money, which can translate to selling themselves to another company, outsourcing work, and eliminating employees. It happens every day. When a company is sold, merges, or is acquired in some way, one of the first corporate cost-cutting tasks is to map out talent pools within the firm, looking for duplication and redundancy.

Suppose your company is acquired by another firm and you're in accounting. The acquiring company already has an accounting department. As in war, to the victor goes the spoils, and suddenly your job is at risk—through no fault of your own. A person can go from feeling secure to being unemployed in an incredibly short time. None of us like the insecure feeling of being on thin ice, but unless you pay attention to reality you could face disaster. You must take steps to manage your career every day.

In fact, this management approach should cover your entire life. If something's important in your life, manage it. Unfortunately, most people spend far more time managing their relationships, investments, blood pressure, and stamp collection than their careers? Why is that?

Do you think just going to work and doing a good job is enough? Not even close.

Managing your career isn't difficult in most cases. All it takes is keeping your eyes and ears open to absorb all you see and hear. Pay attention to the grapevine, listen to what those you trust are saying—and notice what they're doing. Managing your career means if you leave a position, you leave it on your terms; not on the terms of organizational whim or judgment. For example, if the professional services group is shrinking and people are either transferring to other departments or leaving the company, these changes should trigger a response from you. Does it make sense to be the last one there? If you believe you're at risk, can you look at other positions within the organization and see if there's a possibility for internal movement? That type of move can be strategically brilliant, especially if you identify and secure a position that creates more value for the organization than the position you currently occupy. In these financially difficult times, the right move internally can make a big difference in your stability within the organization.

Another way to manage your career from within is to identify a problem you can handle, and then resolve it. Solve the problem, and unless it's absolutely obvious, be sure to mention you're the one who saved the day. Remember, if you add value, you must ring your own bell now and then. Do it nicely, professionally, and in good taste but you must be sure to ring it. This is the opposite of what most people do in a bad economy. They remain quiet, stay hidden, do their jobs, and hope the axe doesn't fall. That approach is not a good way to manage your career. You need to be visible—seen as someone who's doing everything possible to add value to the organization during these tough times. As a rule, the more value you bring to the table, the more difficult it is to make you a part of the layoff. (Corporate speak is "whacked" or "shot;" interesting choice of the vernacular, yes?)

Almost everyone who's working knows of some thorny problem they can tackle if they want to apply themselves. I suggest you consider doing just that. Highly visible problems are better than less visible ones. Also, fixing problems that will make those in positions of power smile is the best tactic. I want you playing this game to win.

One more concept. Every business has one problem that never goes away: they need more dollars coming in the door. If you ever have the ability to bring business to your organization by making introductions or opening doors, use your influence to do so. Nothing is more valuable than employees who are rainmakers. Even if this intervention isn't part of your job, it will be appreciated and remembered.

If you're worried about your position, you may be tempted to approach your boss and ask if your job is secure. To those who are proactive, this seems like a reasonable thing to do as opposed to sitting around, hoping for the best. But even if you have an excellent relationship with your boss, approaching him about your job security may not be a sound approach, for two reasons: First, he probably can't tell you the truth, due to endless reasons that range from legal issues to timing and logistics. A layoff has to be done professionally and correctly, with all things carefully planned out to the last degree. It's usually top secret until the ax falls. Secondly, your boss may not know the answer. In fact, he may be laid off first.

Generally speaking, asking if you'll be laid off disturbs the appropriate order of events made by people who are orchestrating the layoff. Honestly, what do you expect your boss to say? "Yes, you'll be laid off in 30 days." Then what? I advise you to forget about asking that question.

Managing your career also means looking outside your own company as well. Not only are you part of a specific firm; you belong to a larger industry. Manage your career inside and outside your organization. Keep one ear to the ground, paying attention to what the rest of the world is doing and how this news relates to your industry and your profession within that industry. Look for trends, opportunities, and any other information that will help you to manage your future.

If you fail to manage your future, either your employers will do it for you or you'll remain on cruise control, unaware of potential danger ahead.

In the first scenario things might work out, but your future growth will always come in second behind the needs of the organization. I personally like to be in the driver's seat, and I believe it's best for you to be there as well. In the second scenario, you're depending upon luck to have things work out for the best. This is a dangerous plan, and I hope I can convince you it's better to rely on skill and insight than the hand of fate.

Please, if you aren't managing your career, begin to do so now.

Chapter 15
Animal House is Extinct

*"College is the best time of your life. When else are your parents
going to spend several thousand dollars a year just for you
to go to a strange town and get drunk every night?"*
—David Wood

The New College Student

This hard-nosed chapter is written for two specific groups of readers: high school seniors ready to embark on a four year jaunt through college, and the parents of these students who will probably be paying the bills.

For openers, a college degree, even well earned, is no longer a guarantee of finding the best possible job after graduation. Truth be told, it isn't a guarantee of finding *any* job after college. That's the sad reality of life in America today. On the other hand, a good education accompanied by a degree will never hurt—and does give you a head start. Your degree will be a great asset and is often a stone cold requirement in the search for employment. Therefore, if you're going to embark upon the college experience you should strive for the best possible education.

At one time in our history, college seemed to mostly consist of the Animal House model: binge drinking, casual sex, and sleeping till noon, followed by last minute cramming in a desperate attempt not to get tossed out. The world has changed, and those stoner days are gone. Thomas L. Friedman's book *The World is Flat*[7] showed us the entire world is connected, propelling us into a hyper-competitive global society. Technology and new ideas have changed everything. You'll be hired for that first job based on how well you applied yourself in college, what you accomplished there, and the value you can bring to an organization. You'll be expected to contribute at a high level every day. The time to grow up is before you enter college, not after you graduate.

The fact that you're able to attend college places you in a privileged class. If you don't recognize that, then you are self-indulgent and filled with an irritating sense of entitlement. Despite what you may believe, a four year college degree costing in the six figures is not part of your false sense of entitlement nor your inflated self-worth. Going to college is a privilege and an opportunity, not a birthright.

Let's look at the cost of college. If you're paying for school through loans and grants, and the total amount doesn't worry you, allow me to sound a wake-up call. Shelling out $100,000 to $200,000 with the intent of going on a four year joy ride makes you big time dumb. Surely you can see that paying for something you don't intend to maximize is moronic.

Too many people spend four years of their lives and pay a small fortune to get a degree, when what they should be getting is an education. They slide by with just the minimum amount of effort required to graduate. They spend a ton of money and receive a tiny amount of education, all for the privilege of behaving like a child for four more years.

College is big business. Only suckers fork over that kind of cash and accept little return on investment with a boozy smile.

I'll be blunt: you are not going to college to sleep in your own puke and post drunken pics of yourself on Facebook. You need to get an education and prepare to enter the world of work.

The good news here is that you can do great things and still have fun in college, if you learn to achieve a balance. I strongly suggest you define and embrace a way of living that supports your primary objective: to learn as much as possible and get a great education. This won't be accomplished if you cave in to peer pressure and bad behavior.

> If you're attending college you're an adult, and it's time to act like one.

Have fun, but do great things. Make contacts, ask questions, and reach out to the new and the different. Read and study. Learn to program. Pick a foreign language, and learn it well. Network like crazy. This is your chance to launch a solid foundation for a great career and a fruitful life. The freedom to pursue your dreams with such abandon and freedom may never come again. Attempting to be cool by following the crowd is a fool's existence. Always put business before pleasure, get the best grades humanly possible and by the beginning of your junior year, begin thinking about what you'll do after college. Do you know someone who's too dumb to understand this? Help them see the light and you may change a life.

A special note to parents: Two things!

First, if you decided to buy your kid a car, would you choose a Ferrari? Probably not. I suggest you use that same logic when selecting a college for your son or daughter. I've met parents who say, "I'll send my kid to any school she wants to attend." This is often a bad idea. I have a friend who chose Brandeis University at $51,000 per year over a state school at $23,000 per year because, in the end, he liked the Brandeis campus more. That is absurd. For your kid to go to a top tier school and wind up with a 2.6 GPA and a degree in cultural anthropology is just plain silly. How does that prepare them for the world of work? I strongly advise you to match your child with a school that's appropriate, affordable, and a match for his capabilities and aspirations.

Second, I strongly encourage a state school. Not good enough for your kid because she intends to do brilliant things in college? Not good enough for your son, because he got straight A's in high school? Perfect! Let him become the valedictorian of a state school and go on from there. Should some kids enroll in top tier schools? Of course, but only when a solid, specific reason for doing so is in place. The Ivy League is not for everyone. Don't spend 50 large per year on a school because a kid likes the campus. Spend your money wisely.

When it comes to keeping tabs on your son or daughter at school, if you're the parent footing the bill, then it's your money and your investment. I suggest you treat this as an investment without allowing love to cloud your judgment. If your kid is flunking out, work with him to fix the problem, or pull him out and reconsider the college decision. Throwing good money after bad won't help either of you.

Dean Wormer had it right: fat, lazy, and stupid is no way to go through life. It's also no way to go through college.

Chapter 16

The Recent Graduate

*"The hey day when a high school or college education would serve
a graduate for a lifetime is gone. Today's recipients of diplomas
expect to have many jobs and to use a wide range of skills
over their working lives."*

—Alan Greenspan

*T*o get a good job, you need to get a good education."
That quote was the byword of people who sold higher
education to students like me—and it was mostly true. When
I entered college there was little question about the merits of a
good education. Life was simple. If you wanted a good job, you
got the best possible education, and that was the end of it. During
junior year you began looking for a job or career. You pushed a bit
harder during the senior year, sending out resumes and occasionally
visiting the career center.

Somehow you landed that first job and you were on your way.
Life seemed reasonable. With little extra effort, you became a
responsible citizen with a job. The alternative was the draft board,
waiting to sign you up if you weren't otherwise occupied with
college. Education was the answer; end of conversation. A good
education equaled a good job.

We don't need statistics to tell us the world has dramatically changed since those days, but here's just one: According to a survey by the National Association of Colleges and Employers, employers planned to hire 22 percent fewer graduates in the spring of 2010. I doubt 2011 will be much better, and I believe 22 percent is a low estimate. Furthermore, starting salaries were down for the graduating class of 2010; a sad backward slide for those who are lucky or skilled enough to find a position. In all of my years of recruiting, I've never received so many resumes and calls for help. People I know and people I've never met are constantly asking me to help point a recent college grad in the right direction.

A degree no longer guarantees a job. In many cases it doesn't even guarantee an interview.

Twenty years ago companies hired people to travel the country doing college recruiting. I remember it well, because I often rode along with those folks to help them land the best students. My role was to help graduating students clearly understand our company and how we could help them realize their dreams. Students were wooed by one employer one day, another the next, and then they'd make visits to the organizations, complete with tours, back slapping, and handshakes. Ball games and dinner made for lots of fun all around. Offer letters would go out, parents were called, promises were made, and life seemed rosy.

Those were great times, and I thought they'd go on forever. Today, college recruiting still happens, but things are no longer simple. For example, what about students who have a degree in English literature coupled with minor in business and a GPA of 2.9? Do you think education will get them a good job and a stable career?

What does all this mean to you or your kids? Five talking points:

College Isn't the Answer for Everyone

My son did so poorly in high school that while they were lining up the band for the graduation march—of which he was the band leader—they were still trying to figure out if he'd completed enough of his work to graduate. Playing three-card monte with homework assignments and tests almost cost him his diploma. My son, and I love him dearly, is not college material. He went on to languish in retail for a year and hated it. He joined the Navy at 19 and now at almost 35 is the most responsible guy I've ever met. He receives a good salary and has gained the respect of peers. If he stays in for the full twenty years, he'll receive senior officer level benefits for life. He ended up in a wonderful career in the most technical space the Navy has to offer, but once again, he was not college material, and he'll be the first to tell you so.

Remember when you were in high school—how easy it was to identify the kids who didn't want to be there? I mean the ones with aloof attitudes, counter culture styles, and lack of interest in anything academic. They had no interest in learning, nor did they want to sit there and be bored by all the things in life they didn't give a damn about. They wanted out—and I believe that was their right. After a certain age, if kids truly want to leave school we need to let them do just that. It's a travesty to push them into a college where they'll accomplish little, while their parents pay the tuition.

The only ones benefiting from such an arrangement are the institutions of higher learning—schools that tuck away significant dollars and confer too many degrees to the unwilling and the barely educated. Once again, college is not for everyone. You may find this sad and unfair, but as with everything else in life, we need to deal with reality, not dreams.

I know a guy named Bill Gates who wasn't terribly interested in college either. He dropped out, but fortunately he seems to be well adjusted and is making a few dollars here and there.

Got An MBA?

According to Roger M. Martin, the MBA is by far the leading degree in American postgraduate education. More than a quarter of all postgraduate students pursue MBAs. As I see it, the MBA has replaced the Bachelors Degree as the de facto "nice to have" for a position in business. At times I wonder if this planet needs even one more MBA, because I see a ton of those folks who still cannot get jobs. Is it good to run out and get one? Perhaps. More education is a good thing, but will it guarantee a great job? I believe in most cases the answer is "no."

More than three-quarters of master's programs responding to a recent Graduate Management Admission Council survey reported their applications declined last year. More remarkably, 41 percent reported that applications were down more than 20 percent. Will an MBA help? Perhaps, but my money is on grit, native intelligence, strong people skills, and other intangibles that represent perceived value.

I believe the MBA has fallen victim to the standard American belief that more is somehow better. If one cheeseburger is good, are 12 cheeseburgers better? Beware of spending the time and the money on an MBA without doing extensive research on your particular situation, industry, and expectations. Extending your education when you don't need to may be a mistake.

I've already pointed out the fact that the social contract between education and getting a good job was broken long ago, and expecting it to come back anytime soon is unrealistic. In the past, this contract made sense on some level because we didn't have to worry about competition from recent graduates from India or China who seemed smart beyond anything we've ever seen. We used to compete with the kids from the next town or the next state.

Now, in our very flat world, you compete with kids from across the globe, most of whom don't get summers off or endless vacations. They are scary smart—and they want your job.

Competition is now international, and many come to that competition with talent, educational credentials, brains, and drive that is absolutely breathtaking. I can't imagine how the United States will ever return to our former position as dominant educational leader.

*As an aside, an article in the Wall Street Journal of 1-8-11 points to results from the Student International Assessment, a test given every 3 years to determine rankings for 15-year-old students. The areas for testing are math, reading and science. American results? Feel free to draw your own conclusions. Math ranking, 31st. Reading ranked 17th and science ranked 23rd.

Is an education going to help you land a job? In most cases, the answer is yes. On the other hand, as stated by Louis Menand in a recent article in *The New Yorker*, the college education from which some 1.5 million people will graduate this year is basically a "sleepover with grades." Honestly, can it get any more depressing than that?

"A sleepover with grades."

This is a sad assessment of what we've become. Want my advice? If you go to college, get an "A" in every single subject humanly possible. Drinking, parties and hooking up? Far and few between, and only after you've studied a lot. Bottom line on a degree? It's a great pursuit and it will certainly help. Will your degree guarantee a job? I seriously question it.

Air Conditioning and Refrigeration?

Want a job? Why not go into one of the trades? Why not become a carpenter, a builder of homes, or a plumber? I assure you the money is reasonable and opportunities are always there. You can work for others, work for yourself, build a company, or be a one-person show. Is air conditioning and refrigeration school a less than noble pursuit? Personally, I think not. The time has come for making

* http://nces.ed.gov/surveys/pisa/

practical decisions. Whimsy, possibility thinking, and optimism aren't an iron clad recipe for success. Might your son, daughter, or you go to college, earn a degree, join a company, and have a great career? Of course—that's entirely possible. Unfortunately, things don't always turn out that way. Has the time arrived for more practical considerations that will help our young people transition from home to adulthood and be self-sufficient? I suspect so, but once again, the choice is yours. Please choose carefully. As a parent, I too want my son to do great things, but we all need to recognize that many different roads can lead to greatness.

Let me tell you a story. I once recruited for a large employer in Idaho. I did most of my work from Boston, but I flew into Idaho once a month for a week and stayed in a great hotel in Idaho Falls. My first week in Idaho was tough for me, because I had to adjust to a new culture and climate, where the Italian restaurants were none too good. Part of my work was trying to understand why so many people who were employed with this company for over 20 years stayed on so long. Most of them had traveled west with the intention of staying for two years or so and then returning back home. Twenty years later, many were still living in Idaho with kids, wives, homes, and careers. Why did they stay?

Fast forward three months and it was an entirely new deal for me. I began to see the light. I knew my way around, the social scene was far better than expected, I made a few friends, and Idaho Falls was, to my way of thinking, fantastic. It was like living two different lives; one in Boston with my family, and one in Idaho. Would I have relocated there for the right position? Under the right circumstances, yes, and I'm hardly an open-minded person when it comes to moving.

Recent graduates who won't relocate fascinate me. Why be unwilling to look at a position that might be exactly the opportunity you're hoping to land? The world is getting smaller and we must adjust. I do understand relocation is an individual decision based upon many factors and variables. All I'm suggesting is that if you truly want an opportunity, try to keep an open mind about how moving could benefit you in the long run. Do you enjoy living in San Francisco, and you don't feel good at the thought of going to Tennessee fresh out of school? I understand the desire to remain with the comfortable and the chic, but taking a risk and moving might be the best thing you ever did for your career. I also urge you to realize that nothing is forever. If you're unhappy, you can always find another place to live, or even go home again.

> I urge you to be brave and understand the power of taking a risk—the power of saying "yes" to opportunity.

I realize the transition from college to the world of work can be challenging, even in the best of times. I have grave concern for new graduates who'll be making that leap in these difficult times. My best advice is to be creative, open yourselves to different possibilities, and be prepared to take risks. This will maximize your opportunity for success and allow new and different possibilities to enrich your life.

Chapter 17

Gornish

"What we need now are more people who specialize in the impossible."
—Kenny More, co-author of
The CEO and the Monk

*N*o sense looking it up: I can tell you what it means right here. According to the dictionary, Gornish "is most often used to indicate a sensation of profound profundity." I hope you will consider the following concepts that are too short for entire chapters but too important to be omitted from this book. I believe these thoughts will help you develop a heightened awareness regarding the world of work and how to achieve your professional goals.

You Have Nothing

Here's what you might hear at some point in the interviewing process. It may come from the HM, from someone in Human Resources, or a host of other places:

"We see you as a great candidate for the position."

"This has been an excellent talk. You'd be great for this position."

"I'm sure we'll be making you an offer next week. I just need some signatures to get this done." (known as "sigs" in the biz.)

"I'll be sending you an offer letter on Tuesday."

This is exciting stuff; music to your ears. Your heart soars, and you walk to your car on a cloud of optimism and hope. The time to put a down payment on that Lamborghini has arrived. Finally, you've landed a job and life is like one big party with ice cream and cake.

I hate to break up your party, but here it comes. Ready?
You have nothing.

Sure, you just received a few uplifting words, but that's all you have. Until you actually hold an offer letter in your hand, you have absolutely, positively nothing. *Zero.* Anything can go wrong when it comes down to actually getting the offer letter in your hands. If I had a dime for every time I saw something go awry at the last minute, I'd be rich. Shaky budgets and fat cat sigs that sit on desks for weeks on end can kill your offer before it becomes reality. Position changes, frozen requisitions, organizational realignment, and endless other snags can prevent even the best intentioned companies from making that offer. Unfortunately, this is all part of the confusion, politics, and turmoil of getting your offer out the door. It's a sad reality of the entire hiring process.

The only time you ever have anything of real value is when you hold the offer letter in your hands—official and signed. Therefore, you need to maintain your job search momentum.

Do not slow down for even one day, based upon the promise of an offer. If you fail to take this advice and buy into the heady promise of an ephemeral offer, you'll be making a classic mistake. You put job hunting activity on the back burner and wait. And wait. And wait a bit more. This is not a good thing. If you choose to stop all activity and wait for an alleged offer to fall into your hands, it will cost you in a big way. It will cost you in time lost and productivity diminished. You'll lose the forward motion and thrust you've worked to build during your search. Worst of all, when the promised job falls through, you'll feel as though you're starting your quest all over again. To make matters worse, many people feel a sense of being victimized; of being screwed out of an offer for reasons they will never know or understand. Please don't let this happen to you.

Do you have the *promise* of an offer? That's great. Let the company move forward on getting that offer letter into your hands. Meanwhile, keep up the search as though you have nothing— because that's exactly what they gave you. Perhaps that job will indeed become a reality, and for your sake, I hope so. Worst case scenario? You'll get a real offer from another company. With a second offer, people are actually competing for you as an employee. Now you have a choice to make; an embarrassment of riches, so to speak. Can you imagine having two or even three offers to consider? Is that such a bad thing? I think not. Be happy for the promise of an offer, but do not stop your job search.

Make Yourself Uncomfortable

No, you didn't misread that heading. I mean what I said. I want you to feel the awkwardness of doing things outside your comfort zone. I want you to get uncomfortable. Those of us who avoid discomfort don't grow or change. Please, make yourself uncomfortable, and keep doing it until you feel more at ease in such a place. Let's look at a few examples.

Are you uncomfortable speaking in front of a group? So am I, but I made an extra effort to learn about public speaking. Are you uncomfortable writing an article? I used to be, but after a lot of practice and a bit of rejection, the articles found their way into print, and later online. Now writing articles and speaking in public are second nature and a necessary part of all I do to be successful. Do you feel uncomfortable taking the lead on a project because it's a stretch? Perfect. Begin that stretch as soon as possible. You have no idea how far you can go unless you reach out of your comfort zone to explore new and unfamiliar activities

Does running a meeting attended by peers and managers make you nervous? Does taking the lead make you feel insecure? Do it anyway. Look at people who are doing things you want to do. Study what they've accomplished and how they did it. Learn all you can about them. Ask questions. Even if you don't know them well, take a risk and ask how they achieved success. Some may not tell you, but most will be flattered by your request and more than happy to help. Listen and learn. Follow their lead and adopt the things that led to their success. Incorporate new parameters into the flight path you've logged for yourself.

If a person you approach doesn't have time to coach you, find someone who will. Be unstoppable in your quest to grow and change professionally. If you push hard and don't give up, the results will amaze you.

Are you concerned because your results may not be perfect? Not to worry, because I guarantee they won't be. My results aren't perfect either. This book is not perfect. Will it be criticized? Perhaps, but I don't care. Will my future presentations and efforts at leadership and creating meaningful value and content be perfect? Hardly, but I'll make a damn good effort.

The best we can do needs to be good enough. Perfect is out of the question. I suggest you try hard, aim for excellence, and let that satisfy you. World peace does not depend on your presentation, article, or book. Do what needs to be done, go home, and be happy with what you have accomplished. Are you afraid someone might laugh at you, say they've read better articles, or fall asleep during your meeting? Who cares? Can you see how easy it is to sit in the audience and be critical? Let them get out of the chair and give it a try. Allow me to tell you a secret: most people will encourage your efforts and applaud your success.

> I urge you to get comfortable with being uncomfortable.
> Come face to face with your fear and do not blink. This
> new behavior and attitude will pay tremendous dividends
> in terms of accomplishments and rewards.

You'll become a better person for stepping out of your comfort zone and taking a shot at the things you need to master. Feeling uncomfortable yet?

Know What's Expected

At one time I was consulting for a large software company and we managed to hire a great engineer for a hard-to-fill position. The search took much longer than expected, but we were all delighted with the new hire—a bright guy from a big company, who understood the technology and had the experience and education we needed. I saw him in the halls occasionally, and we chatted a bit. I asked if all was well, and he told me things were great. This was wonderful. In a world where everyone being happy is a rarity, we all felt fine with this new hire.

Fast forward six months. The hiring manager came to my office, looking unhappy. When we closed the door to discuss things, he told me the new engineer wasn't doing anything. Nothing. I was stunned.

"How is that possible?" I asked. This fellow was the first one in the office every day and the last to leave. He never left his desk. He lived on the computer. How could he not be doing anything?

I left the manager in my office and went to see the employee. He was exactly where I expected him to be: at his computer, working. I closed the door. He looked at me. I looked at him. He smiled. I smiled. We talked a bit, and I probed gently as to what he did all day. He gave me some answers, but they didn't ring true. He knew it and I knew it. He didn't know what to say or how to account for how he spent his time. Suddenly, it dawned on me that, shocking as it was, I knew the exact nature of the problem.

Here is the conversation that followed when I decided to get straight to the point and play on my hunch:

"You have no idea what your job is, do you?" I asked.

"Absolutely none," he said. "Not even a clue."

"Tell me," I said, "what do you do here all day?"

He put his fingers on the keyboard and did the alt/tab cool key combo. "I play Solitaire," he said. "I do it all day."

I opened my mouth to speak, but nothing came out. I was beyond shocked. How could this possibly happen?

He folded his hands on his lap and stared straight ahead. We were quiet. I looked at him and began laughing. He looked at me and joined in the laughter. That was an amazing moment.

Strange as it seems, no one had ever told this new employee what was expected of him, so he never did anything. He went to meetings and listened, spoke occasionally, and then went back to his computer to play Solitaire. The interview covered questions of deep technology, shared programming languages, and past experiences in the mainframe world. Multiple interviews followed, and it was determined the candidate was well qualified. But they never disclosed exactly what was expected of this new employee, and so he slipped through the cracks. Embarrassed about seeming to be foolish in the eyes of his team, he never actually asked what they wanted him to accomplish in terms of deliverables. The days turned to weeks and to months as he tried to look busy.

This is not an isolated story. I often see employees who don't understand exactly what's expected of them. They may do a lot of work, but not necessarily the work they were hired to do. This isn't a good place to be, so please don't let it happen to you.

The bottom line to all of this is simple. If you aren't sure what's expected of you, ask early in the process. If you wait until you're hired, it's almost too late, because you're locked into a position containing deliverables with which you're unfamiliar. We're all well aware of the fact that positions have an associated profile, usually covered in a brief summary. But these documents can be vague, out of date, or a conglomeration of thoughts from a host of well-intentioned managers who tried to make some contribution to the profile. Sadly, many employees who accept new positions are in the dark about what's expected of them. They might understand the nature of the job, but not its actual deliverables.

It's critical that the person being hired receives a clear, definitive understanding of what's expected and, if possible, how results will be measured. As an employee, you should ask your manager in no uncertain terms to list the three or four most important things he'll expect of you. Then write them down. Only through the focused interpretation of your hiring manager will you develop a clear, definitive understanding of exactly what you need to do. If the job seems overwhelming and the list endless, ask for priorities so you know what's most important to your manager. You'll have a greater chance of success if you know your manager's priorities instead of sitting around trying to figure them out.

> Remember, your first responsibility and the first line of action for success is always the same: keep your bosses' boss off your bosses' back.

If your first priority in life is getting the job you want, that priority should quickly shift once you've been hired. Your new focus should be keeping the job—and that means you need to know exactly what's expected of you. Lack of qualification and experience usually aren't the issues for people who do poorly in a job and lose it. Hiring managers quickly weed out candidates whose lack of experience will lead to poor job performance. What's far more difficult is getting the manager and new employee to work together effectively in a way that meets the manager's expectations.

As the employee in this arrangement, trying to guess what's expected of you is high risk behavior and can be a dangerous road to travel. If you understand this, you'll be far ahead of the curve, will come up to speed faster, and perform at a more effective level. When you know exactly what's expected of you, there is potential for great things to happen.

What's Next?

Looking for work is a cascade of events that must be managed on both the macro and micro level. You are the chief strategist and the tactical person as well. Everything that happens is up to you: perhaps an exchange of casual e-mails at first, then a phone screen or an interview, that might lead to a request for references. Each of these events has a starting point and an ending point. We always need to remember that we're the ones who must drive the process. To do this, we must always know the answer to one question: What's the next step? The next step may be evident based upon conversation and circumstance, but sometimes it's difficult to know where you stand. I strongly suggest you ask it as a question.

Example: "Thank you for seeing me today. What's the next step in the process?"

As the driver, it's vitally important you end that phone screen, the interview, and any other step with an understanding of what comes next. Armed with this information, you have time to prepare for the coming event. Knowing what comes next also puts a bit of healthy pressure on the people with whom you're interviewing. For example, if they have no idea what the next step might be, this gives them a reason to think it over.

Knowing what comes next opens an opportunity to ask other questions. For example, if the next step is to meet with the VP of marketing, you can inquire about that person. You might even go so far as to ask if you should bring a presentation. Honestly, unless you ask a totally dumb question, any inquiries you make will yield something of value you can use for the upcoming event. Knowledge is power.

Find out exactly what the next step in the process might be, and feel free to ask more questions to derive further information. Getting a job is a process. Do all you can to keep the process from stalling, because getting a job is what those in the agency business call "doing a deal," and sadly, time kills all deals.

> Show me a deal that has been dragging on for nine months, and I'll show you a deal that is not going to happen.

Age Discrimination

I'm reminded of a line in the Emmy nominated short story entitled *They're Tearing Down Tim Riley's Bar* written by Rod Sterling in the late 1960s. The line is spoken by the main character, Randolph Lane, to a much younger man, Harvey Doane, who was after Mr. Lane's job. Lane turns to Doane and says; "Why don't we level with one another? I'm on the way down. You're on the way up, and we're just passing each other in midair. I'm looking at a threat and you're looking at an obstacle." This is a poignant study of what we are as a country and a people. Rod Sterling doesn't show a pretty image of us, but it's a stunning piece of work, and you won't be sorry if you read it.

Age is no problem if you're 28, but it certainly becomes an issue if you're 48—or even worse, 58. As a society, we have little use for those who age in the workplace. They can be replaced at half of the cost on most days by the eager, the willing, and the young. No need to hang onto the older guy with the thinning hair or the woman who can't move as quickly as she once did. Replace them with a newer model and be done with it. Where they go and what they do is not your concern, because they committed the ultimate crime: they ceased to be young, and in this country that is unforgivable.

Age discrimination is a monster problem in this country. I can go on endlessly about the corrosive effect is has on everything from creativity and diversity in the workplace to our society in general, but that isn't within the scope of this book. On the other hand, I do need to touch upon age discrimination, because the over-40 person looking for a job will surely feel its effects. Ageism can creep into the workplace for any of us, but it's most heavily felt by the baby boomers.

Unfortunately, there's little you can do about people who see you as too old and won't hire you. If you're thinking you can sue them, I suggest that's a fool's errand. A far better course of action is to go out and find another organization that sees your value.

I can't make you, or myself, any younger, but I can make suggestions. For openers, you should maintain your dignity and be proud of what you've accomplished in life. I can safely suggest you do not dye your hair black; it will look silly. I hope you don't get plastic surgery, because that isn't a meaningful solution. Lying about your age presents not only legal issues, but is an affront to the basic dignity and self-respect you earned by remaining alive and productive for so long.

Can you even imagine telling someone you're ten years younger so they'll feel better about hiring you? That is an unspeakable solution.

I do suggest you take good care of yourself, remain upbeat, and let your accomplishments speak for themselves. If you've been around this planet for a long time, then you've seen a lot. Use this to your advantage and make your experience work for you. Mentor the next generation and lead by example. Push the boundaries of what's possible with your judgment and your strength. Model integrity and encourage others through your words and actions. If you can do this, you'll stand out as a valued professional. Honestly, what more can you hope to achieve?

Armed with this information and insight, it is my sincere hope that those who have been displaced will use the frustration and yes, perhaps even the rage, to drive forward and look for employment with a new set of eyes—with an enhanced vision of what's important and a renewed sense of purpose. I ask you to remain optimistic and keep hope alive.

I just returned from having lunch with a friend who was out of work for 21 months. He landed a new position, put the misery and adversity behind him, and is on the road to being successful again. After three months of employment, he tells me his long stretch of unemployment seems like a bad dream and he rarely thinks of it. I applaud him for this attitude, because looking forward is a strong attribute of those who survive the hard times. He did it by employing courage, creativity, and a strong belief that the future was going to be bright. I know you can do this as well.

Chapter 18
My Story

"The miserable have no other medicine but hope."
—Friedrich Nietzsche

*M*y father died in May of 2008.

I mention this here because, like you, I have a story—a deeply personal story, and I wish to share a bit of it with you. I want you to understand I am no different from you, and on many levels, I can feel your pain and your anguish. Pain is, to a great degree, the reason I wrote this book.

I see this book as more than just insight and opinion into our current professional standing. It's more than a simple treatise on unemployment and loss of professional standing—on reasoning and resumes. It's about the lives we lead and the things we feel during that miserable period of time. It's a book that touches on all the ills, the misery, and the injustices with which we must live. As I reread my work aloud, I see it as a work that seethes at times: a manifesto that speaks to the fact that life without work, for most people, is a greatly diminished existence. Their lives are compromised; watered down in the places where real meaning and deep satisfaction once existed. Commitment and attention to detail have been stolen from our days—replaced by the ability to sleep late and be up till all hours of the night. Want to read till 4 a.m.? Feel free, because you don't have to get up for work in the morning. This new life is far less useful then it used to be, because of the gnawing sense that something important is missing from our day-to-day existence. Worse than that, we can't seem to fix it as we did in the past. We go from one day to the next with the hope that something will magically happen tomorrow; with the belief that life will tell us, "Here you go. All better now?" So we hope, and we wait, and we hope.

I've felt it in my own life, and I hate it. Furthermore, I see it in the faces, the rhythm, and the meanderings of people whose existence touches mine every day. Freud said, "There are only two things in life; love and work. In the absence of either, there can only be neurosis." When I was single and employed, I scoffed at this aphorism. I take it far more seriously now. Back in the day, I was absolutely bulletproof. Today, that illusion is gone. The belief that "everything will be all right" is a lovely memory of times gone by. A close friend told me his favorite thing used to be his day off—the one day a week away from work that allowed him to sleep in a bit and do things he could remember fondly during his daily commute as he traveled to work. He hasn't worked for well over a year as of this writing, and having a day off is now meaningless.

I think of my other friends: John and Hubert and Scott, plus endless others. No work and no jobs for so long. It makes me want to weep, but I don't do that, because if I start weeping I might not stop. I see the mill where Digital Equipment Corporation once employed over 125,000 people at its high water mark. Gone. Not a scrap or a corner of a memo remains of that grand organization. Just ghosts in the halls of this large cut up mill that now contains endless smaller companies who struggle for survival every single day. The annual Digital reunion is still hosted here, and former employees eyeball each other while trying to reconcile the older battle-scarred versions to the young, invincible, and vibrant person they once knew. "Look over there; is that so and so? Are you sure?" The entire scene depresses me so I leave my office early to avoid it. The old Digital parking lot is mostly empty these days as well. New tenants use only a fraction of the space. Before the crash two years ago, you needed to take the bus to the overflow lot if you arrived for work past 8:30 a.m. Now you can slide in whenever you like. There is no bus because the overflow lot is nearly empty. There used to be no parking spaces on Main Street, and if you parked for more than two hours, you were given a citation—even if you fed the meter. Where the hell is everyone? The excitement and fun, the electricity and the crackle are gone. It's like midnight on Main Street today. Can you for a moment imagine the lives and the feelings of those who once inhabited those spaces? I can.

The second reason I mention my father's death is to tell you of my own naiveté. My expectation was that life would somehow be on hold until this employment problem was resolved; that I would only have to deal with one misery at a time while I rectified my employment situation. I was so very wrong.

Want to keep reading? This story doesn't get any better. After my father died, my primary and lucrative contract suddenly ended when the company for which I was recruiting was purchased by another. I was out. I of course had no idea the economy was melting down as severely or as quickly as it was. I had no idea this would be a forever type of a deal. As such, I remember thinking it was nice to have a short break to do some writing, but that was only the beginning of my personal nightmare. Unemployment compensation helped a bit, but I hated that existence. The folks at the unemployment office were nice, but I only went one or two times because I found the entire scene so demoralizing.

A few months after my job vaporized, my wife lost her job as a corporate recruiter with a Fortune 100 company. This was heartbreaking because she is so good at what she does and so committed to her craft. It was unfair and wrong. The situation was devoid of anything one could call an upside. All I could feel was rage as I saw her struggle to find work in a world that was shedding recruiters like crazy. After all, if you're laying off endless employees, what use would you have for a recruiter? Over-supply and no demand. It was like a fire sale as the recruiting industry was decimated.

Two months later, someone close to me went into the hospital for anxiety and depression. The stay was for six weeks, and the experience for my wife and I was horrendous. Here we are, two people who worked all our lives, set adrift with no place to go in the morning and no real purpose for the rest of the day. All we had were hospital visits and conversations over lunch, with nothing to anchor us to the normalcy of life's work and productivity. Three o'clock in the afternoon was as quiet as death. This was getting old fast, and as a person who has little patience, I was not doing well.

I remember getting the bill for life insurance and thinking I was worth more dead than alive. Did I want to be dead? No, I don't think so, but I can assure you being alive wasn't all that much fun either. This realization came from a calm sense of accounting—a summation of the numbers: the mortgage, and the bills. I awakened each day wondering what bad thing would happen next.

The call came in on a Sunday at about 6:00 in the morning as we slept at the Ashworth Hotel in an attempt to get away from it all. I thought I was safe in a hotel. Silly me. I picked up the phone. My wife just stared at me and whispered, "My father?" Yes, it was her father this time. The nurses had just looked in on him, and he smiled at them. They turned around and he was gone. Another funeral. He was a sweet man. Now two fathers gone in less than six months. I was numb.

Interviews were few and far between. We sprayed out resumes like bullets as the world came to an end, with melting housing markets, bailouts of epic proportions, and bad news traveling the airwaves 24 hours a day. We stopped answering the phone. I told my wife, "If someone else dies, the relatives will have to drive over to tell us." We endured a lot of television and reality shows.

Shortly afterward, I remember the day her doctor called with the results of her "routine" chest x-ray. I heard her breathe in. I heard her ask, "So this is how it ends?" In slow motion, this pretty scarecrow with rosy cheeks collapsed and lay crumpled between the door and the wall. It felt like a dream, but it was the beginning of a nightmare.

My wife had a disturbing lesion in her upper right lung. Not too big, and caught through luck and good fortune. I felt coolly detached—frozen with disbelief and terror. After that event, life was broken down into two distinct parts: everything that happened before that day, and all that happened afterward. We tried to convince ourselves it was just a shadow on an x-ray.

I looked to the heavens. What I said isn't printable here, but I remember the threat and the fury: "If you harm one hair on her head; this woman who never hurt anyone in her life. If you hurt her…" It is a haze of disturbing memory as I write this, and I'm still shaken by revisiting this time in our lives.

Doctors and more doctors. Doctors without end. Second opinions. Third opinions. Two surgeries. First to check the margins, which were clean. A second surgery to remove the upper lobe of the right lung. ICU and the holidays at home to recuperate. Neighbors decorate the tree for her. She comes home, sees it, and cries. It was cancer and we got it in time. No chemo. No radiation. It haunts me every single day as we go from scan to scan, searching for pin sized formations in a world we simply wish did not exist.

I was still out of work, with no real sense of things picking up. I was off the charts crazy, or so it seemed then. I would have killed someone if that would change things, but I didn't know who to kill, so I breathed deeply and remained outwardly calm. Days passed. Weeks passed. Somewhere during that time, I remembered to breathe again.

Six months later, my nephew committed suicide. His loss devastated the family. He was 37. We knew he had issues, but this came as a bolt from the blue. The funeral is still a blur. These were the things that happened to other families ... other people. Not to us. But our time had obviously come, and it rolled in with a ferocity I could never have imagined. As a Jew, I joined a Chabad house. I believe they thought I was looking to find God. In a way, I was. Had I been successful, I would have fired six warning shots into his chest.

Listening now, God? I've been trying to get your attention for a long time. Did that get your attention? Tell me, why do bad things happen to good people? Hey God, can you answer that for me?

My wife recovered, but still lives with considerable pain. She is a very brave person.

As I said, life went on despite all the misery. We've endured a difficult two years and look forward to a good 2011. Enough about me. Let's read on as we look to better times ahead and what I believe we must do in to meet the challenges ahead.

Chapter 19
Social Media, Employment, and You

How can you squander even one more day not taking advantage of the
greatest shifts of our generation? How dare you settle for less when
the world has made it so easy for you to be remarkable?"
—Seth Godin

*I*am writing this text on a warm first day of December in the
year 2010. I mention the date for a specific reason—to point
out that this chapter will be the first thing in this book to become
outdated. You need to know and understand that today's technology
will seem almost quaint to us within two years, and ancient in five
years—perhaps sooner. While other ideas in this book will remain
important and essential for a long time, anything written about the
combination of technology and the evolution of our society has a
limited shelf life. In many ways, this is a good thing. The goal of
this chapter isn't to discuss specific social media applications, but to
awaken your mind to the power of social media and the possibilities
for applying it to your specific employment situation. Let's start
with technology.

Technology plays a huge role in our daily lives. We can either
adapt to what technology is currently doing and reap the benefits,
or fail to do so at what will surely become great personal cost. For
openers, let's define Social Media.

"Social media are media for social interaction, using highly accessible and scalable publishing techniques. Social media uses web-based technologies to turn communication into interactive dialogues. Andreas Kaplan and Michael Haenlein[8] also define social media as "a group of Internet-based applications that build on the ideological and technological foundations of Web 2.0, which allows the creation and exchange of user-generated content"[1] Businesses also refer to social media as consumer-generated media (CGM). A common thread running through all definitions of social media is a blending of technology and social interaction for the co-creation of value."   *—Wikipedia*

As Alvin Toffler, the brilliant and renowned futurist stated in his seminal work *Future Shock*, "Technology feeds upon itself."[9] In other words, technology creates and enables more technology, and the curve of acceleration is exponential.

Web 2.0 has arrived, and its impact will continue to change everything at lightning speed. Absolutely, positively, everything. (Please read *Future Shock*. It is frightening, essential, and relevant to our times. I recommend *Catch 22* as well, just for the absurdity of it all.)

You're probably asking, "As a job hunter, why should I care about technology, social media, or what's next?" Because your social survival—economic, educational, and political—depends to a great degree upon your ability to adapt, embrace what's new, and get with the program. The very future of work and our ability to connect with others is rapidly changing. Much of your future success rests upon your ability to develop deep and broad skill sets in areas that have little to do with references and resumes. I see the past world of work vaporizing a bit more every day, while podcasts, Facebook fan pages, texting, and Twitter-related activities increase at breakneck speed. Do you know what a hashtag is? What about search engine optimization? The future is coming, and it's coming fast. We all need to get on this bullet train and ride the wave with effectiveness and grace, or we will become angry and disillusioned people, wondering why others succeed while we do not.

Being effective at older approaches whose time has come and gone does little good for most of us. Today, success often depends not upon strength and determination, but upon our ability to adapt and change. We need to develop a comfort level with the new ways people share information and interact. We need to look for opportunities in ways that are creative and untried. Welcome to the fascinating marriage of technology, economics, and life online. See for yourself how it hampers the progress of people who reject it and supports those who embrace it. Understand its power and its ability to get things done. Join the conversation and contribute to this ongoing evolution—or take your chances while hoping for the best. (Not a good plan.)

Want another reason you should care? Because for many of us, surviving isn't enough. We want rich, fulfilled, and deeply satisfying lives. Mere survival can be a sad, impoverished existence. Honestly, is survival enough for you and your family? Will survival give you the experiences and the exciting journey you seek for your life? I suspect not. If you want more, let's examine the rapid evolution of social media and see how it can help you with employment.

We'll start with three sample aspects of social media that enable users to share and communicate: Facebook, which can be seen as our playground; LinkedIn, which will become our boardroom; and Twitter, an ongoing dialogue for all who wish to join the collective conversation. Personally, I see Twitter, a microblogging platform, as the most effective and deepest reaching of the three. The depth and reach of Twitter, its power and capability, is astonishing. What can YOU say in 140 characters?

Three or four years ago, Facebook, LinkedIn, and Twitter did not exist as they do now. Today, they dominate the Internet, and every forward-thinking person and company on the planet wants to leverage that power to advance their own agendas.

Are you using social media to advance YOUR agenda? Want a new job? A better job? Are you hoping to change careers, relocate from New York to Los Angles, and find a highly rated moving company—all at the same time? You can do this with Twitter alone, and that's just scratching the surface of social media's potential.

What about connectivity? Are you connected? Do you have a smartphone, or is your telephone still attached to a wall plug? Can you connect at a moment's notice if an opportunity presents itself, or do you make people wait an entire day because you aren't wired or only check emails once a week?

The people you *need* will expect you to communicate early and often. Instant communication brings higher expectations of performance, and the bar has been raised for all of us. For example, suppose you're project manager and your resume says you had full responsibility of vendor management for the new wing of a fancy office building in Texas. My client needs pictures of the lower level support brackets before we can sign the contract. They need to see your choice of vendor, and they need to see it *now*. The board meeting is in 20 minutes. Do you have a smartphone to receive this e-mail or text, and then can you just snap a few photos and send them to me? Can you do that in the next five minutes? Or do I wait until you check your phone messages tonight when it's too late and the contract was given to another company? Can you see where this is all going?

My largest target audience for this chapter are baby boomers— the 78 million people born between 1946 and 1964. I can just see some of these folks wagging their fingers in my face and saying, "I don't need the Internet. I can get along just fine without it." Actually, no, you can't.

Though they're identified as the largest generation in recorded history, I see baby boomers as two distinct groups. One segment is active with computers: extremely savvy about the Internet and how it applies to their lives. They didn't have computers back in the day, but they've adapted to understand the technology required to conduct business in today's world. They're up to speed, having successfully made the leap into a wired world. I don't worry about this group.

I do worry about the other group who don't like computers—the ones who won't even consider doing "that Facebook stuff." These are the folks who resist change and have no real understanding of what the Internet and social media can offer. I met a 61-year-old man last week who told me he barely knows how to turn a computer on. Personally, I find this frightening. It's especially sad if you're still in the job market, because you're giving yourself a huge handicap right up front. How can you possibly compete?

Perhaps lack of computer knowledge isn't a problem if you're retired and can spend the day fly fishing, with no need for professional employment. But you're missing out on so much. Going one step further, and not to go all sociologist on you, I believe people who've been around awhile have much to contribute to our global conversation. The lessons they can teach will benefit all of us. Do you know a boomer or senior citizen who'd benefit from learning how to go online, use a computer, and learn about social media? Try to lend a hand if you can.

Eight Insights Into Social Media for Your Review

1. Write a blog. A blog is a shortened version of the word "weblog." This is your own personal place on the Internet to speak your mind and establish an online presence. Software for a blog is free, so it's easy to make all of this happen. You can blog about anything you wish, and doing so will help you begin the process of connecting with the thoughts and ideas of other people online. Understand that your involvement in social media is evolutionary, not revolutionary. This is a marathon, not a sprint, and progress is seldom as dramatic as we might expect.

You probably won't become famous overnight, nor will thousands of people hang on your every word. As the search engines gradually find you online, you'll slowly gain readers and find your niche. A blog is your place to live online. You may post pictures, videos, and other things you wish to share. You're free to accept comments from others, or not. You may comment on other people's blogs, or remain silent. The important thing is to do *something to move this forward.*

If you're seeking employment, I strongly suggest you devote at least part of your blog to your job search. For example, you might post your resume or a biography. You might show samples of your work and provide contact information so people will be able to reach you quickly if an opportunity arises. Here is my contact information, exactly as listed in the Contact page of my personal blog, which is www.employmentrage.com.

Contact

Need to reach me? We can connect in the following ways.

E-mail: howard@employmentrage.com (fastest contact)

Blog: http://www.employmentrage.com

Twitter: @howardadamsky

LinkedIn: http://www.linkedin.com/in/hadamsky

Phone: 617-930-6553

(Not the best way to get me, but it's worth a shot.)

I promise to get back to you as quickly as possible.

Weekends tend to be a bit slower in terms of reaction time.

As you can see, my contact page is simple and to the point but contains several ways to connect with me.

Think of your own blog as a blank slate, where you can do anything you wish with the content. People often tell me they have no idea what to write about in a blog. Last week a friend confided that she had nothing intelligent to say. I find this difficult to believe.

If you're looking for a job, your blog should display value by demonstrating clear thinking and thoughtful opinions.

The blog should highlight your creativity and accomplishments. A blog is a fine place to showcase what you've done and who you are. What more can you possibly want from something that's free, gives you total control of information, and can be accessed instantly from almost any place on the planet?

2. Join and contribute. The Internet is filled with endless groups, forums, and online communities you can join and make part of your professional life. The number of these groups increases daily and the possibilities are as vast as your ability to keep up with everything that interests you. In the beginning, feel free to do what's known as *lurking*—listening and observing quietly without contributing. Doing this gives you a chance to see how others interact, helps you determine the rules and tone of the group, and allows you to decide if this group is for you, or if you need to seek another group. I suggest you look for a good fit and only go to the places in which you feel comfortable. With so many online communities out there, you don't need to be the square peg trying to squeeze into a round hole.

Rules for engagement: Most groups have their own guidelines, but the basic tenets of life on the playground also apply here: play nicely with others, stick to the topics at hand, and if you disagree, do it nicely. Do this and you'll fit in. If others can't seem to follow the rules, consider finding a different group. It's also important to look for reasons and opportunities to help others. If you can offer advice, make introductions, and support other members, you'll soon become a valued contributor. Will everything you do result in a benefit to you? Of course not. That isn't how it works. "Far better to be a kingmaker than a king" has real meaning in the world of social media. The Internet has led me to believe in karma far more than I have in the past. The people I've met are astounding, and the opportunities to become a part of networks continues to amaze me. I hope you become an active participant in the groups that need you and the groups you need. If you do, good things will happen.

3. Don't worry about the numbers. How many Facebook friends do you have? What about LinkedIn connections and Followers on Twitter? Three hundred? Seventeen hundred? Twenty thousand? Is a large number better than a smaller one? Perhaps, to some people, but amassing numbers can be counterproductive. After all, how many people can you keep up with, and what does "keeping up with" actually mean to you? British anthropologist Robin Dunbar explored this concept and found a theoretical limit to the number of people with whom one can maintain a stable social relationship—known as Dunbar's number. That number is around 150, with 230 as the largest possible extension.[10]

Where does it start and where does it end? Is more better? If you have over a hundred thousand people following you on Twitter, can you relate to them in a meaningful way? Many people collect friends and bits of community the way others collected baseball cards in fifth grade. Can you see that sheer numbers may have surface prestige and value, but a look under the hood reveals many other things are more important than numbers: things like the strength of the community you're part of, and its ability to connect you with other communities where you can add value to the conversation. Things like the cooperation and trust that come naturally with the daily ebb and flow of community dialogue. Things like a sense of pride and satisfaction in being able to help others and move everyone's agenda forward, even when there isn't any direct benefit to you. Can you see how numbers are just a slice of the pie? Beware of the big number illusion.

4. Social media and employment. From my unique vantage point of seeing how social media is utilized, I can tell you without a doubt that job hunting and social media are a marriage made in heaven. According to Dan Schawbel, author of the book *Me 2.0: Build a Powerful Brand to Achieve Career Success.* "Between current economic conditions and the technological evolution of the Internet, the traditional approach most job seekers have taken in the past is no longer viable. The approach—developing a resume and cover letter, locating jobs on and submitting your resume to corporate sites and job banks, and crossing your fingers in hopes of receiving a call from a hiring manager—is, for the most part, a thing of the past."[11]

I couldn't say it better myself. Using social media in your employment search can supercharge your opportunities and chances of success. Furthermore, most of this amazing technology and power is FREE and at your fingertips. The possibilities are only limited by your willingness to engage, your ability to connect, and your desire to plug into all that's going on around you. Social media needs to be in your blood. Do not seek a way to tolerate social media; find a way to enjoy it, because this communication method is rapidly becoming the way businesses and people interact.

5. Fear not. Some people are wary of social media because they've heard stories about stalking, invasion of privacy, identity theft, and other negative aspects of the Internet. Many even worry about looking foolish and harming their reputations.

In an article entitled "Fighting the Fear of Social Media," author Curtis Silver says, "When it comes to social media, a lot of individuals and companies are quite afraid. Fear of the unknown. Fear of lack of privacy. Fear of retribution and negative response. Fear of ex-girlfriends' new boyfriends, or of strangers stalking your kids."[12]

If you check Silver's article online, you'll read about a host of ways to calm your fear of the Internet. Personally speaking, I'm not overly brave, but I've never given this a thought. I've been online for endless years, and the worst thing that has ever happened to me is the occasional arrival of more spam than I'd like to receive. No one has stolen my identity, nor has anyone taken my kids. Not only that, but in all my circles of friends and relations, I have never, not one time, heard of anything bad happening to anyone I know. Can something happen in theory? Of course. You see it on television every day, but I believe the odds are on the side of safety, and if you're reasonable about what you put out there, you're unlikely to have a problem. Of course, there's no reason to invite trouble. Are you leaving on a three month vacation? Do you store gold coins in a credenza near the master bath? Putting this info on Facebook for everyone to see isn't exactly a good idea.

Living life well includes taking calculated risks. Most of us go on planes that can crash, drive cars that can skid, and cook with propane canisters that might explode.

If you're afraid of the Internet, you might as well stay in bed all day—and that's no way to live.

People also fear learning new things. As adults, many of us hesitate to expand our horizons because we don't enjoy looking silly while we're struggling to understand how something works. Let me be blunt: if this is your problem, you need to get over it and move on with learning what you need to know. Endless sites on the Internet will help you understand how to send out tweets, the best ways to use LinkedIn, how to connect with your smart phone, cloud computing, and anything else related to social media. I assure you, keeping up with all this isn't exactly easy for me either. I tend to learn things well, but not easily or quickly. I'm currently trying to learn about photography and have had the term "depth of field" explained to me eleven times. I still don't get it, but eventually I will. Please, don't let fear hold you back from learning new things.

6. Understand community. Community can be a difficult concept for newcomers to social media. An online community isn't a place where you occasionally check in and see if you can get people to help you with your business, your book, or the sale of your new weight loss program. A community is not a place where you think of yourself first and everyone else second. A community is a commitment to those around you, where keeping score of who helped whom the most isn't part of the game. Community is global in scope; a place where people conduct business, share ideas, and speak of the possible as well as the impossible with the same degree of enthusiasm and excitement. A community is a place where we go to develop trust as a new and different form of capital. The concept of community is changing rapidly and will continue to evolve. People, in conjunction with technologists, will redefine what is possible as social media pioneers build new and dramatic ways for us to connect, engage, and share. Community exists because we want it to exist. Community is a place to establish identity and value before you need it. A community is a place to give and take value—an opportunity that allows you to be everywhere, doing everything, in far less time than you ever thought possible. A community is the place to be if you want to lift up your spirit and your life while helping others do the same. Les Brown says, "No one succeeds alone." A community is the embodiment of that belief.

Community lives in our hearts and minds, as a spirit of collaboration and good will. No one is forcing you to join and no one forces you to remain.

    7. *Be mindful.* Have you ever done a Google search on yourself? Some people think that's creepy; an ego driven exercise to see how may hits your name will get. Those people are wrong. Doing a monthly Google search of yourself is an important tool in managing your digital shadow. You need to know how you're being presented online—what other people see when they put your name into the Google search box and hit enter. Why is this important? Because Google wants to be the most widely utilized search engine in existence. To do that, they constantly collect information on you, me, and everyone else who uses the Internet. That's why I strongly urge you to be careful what you post. According to Brian Solis, author of the book *Putting the Public Back in Public Relations: How Social Media Is Reinventing the Aging Business of PR* (Co-authored by Deirdre Breakenridge,[13]) "Every tweet, every You Tube video, every image in Flicker, every blog post, every blog comment shows up in Google and it's there for a very long time." [16]

    Can you see the power of things staying out there for others to see for a *very long time?* Do you think people will Google your name if they're serious about hiring you, bringing you on for a contract, leading a workshop—or even dating their sister? Absolutely! I Google everyone. Let me say that again. Everyone. I do it because knowledge is power. I would Google my own mother if necessary. So remember—be mindful when you post. Be careful. Not sure of a post? Wait a day—a full 24 hours—and reread the item before you post. I can't tell you how many times I've decided that a particular post wasn't a good idea, so I didn't pull the trigger. Be mindful of the digital shadow you cast.

8. It's still about people. When Chris Brogan, an extraordinary social media guy, says it's all about people, he's right on the money. Find him online and learn from him.[14] Although the Internet may seem sterile at times, the man/machine interface hasn't removed the essential humanity from our existence. We still need trust, value, and relationships. Social media is about people first, with everything else a distant second. The power of social media allows us to reach out to all who are connected in ways that are quite human and very personal. Treating others in our communities as real people, giving them consideration, sensitivity, and value will open vast new worlds of opportunity, dialogue, and engagement.

Are you looking for a new opportunity related to employment? Let people know. Seek out conversation and interactions related to your quest. Looking to change careers completely? Do you need information about different approaches for your quest? How about insight about how others have succeeded? Social media can support all your efforts in these areas, and more. Just remember to give back more than you take. Chris Brogan shoots for a twelve to one ratio, and I see that as a generous proposition. We are headed for exciting times. I suggest you plug in and join us.

One last point: do not live your life online. Social media can drink up all your time and get in the way of doing other meaningful work involved in seeking employment. The Internet is fun, colorful, and endlessly fascinating. It is without depth, borders, or restrictions. Online content is new and exciting every day, which means it can easily become a major distraction in your life. I strongly suggest you discipline yourself to use social media instead of letting it use you. Even beyond that, I urge you to unplug on a regular basis and be aware of the sights and sounds of life around you.

There are coffee shops in Oregon to experience, barbecue to eat in Dallas, and hot pastrami to dine upon in NYC. (Do not ask for lean pastrami. There is no lean pastrami, so stop asking.) The Brooklyn Bridge is a glorious place to stroll on a warm day in May, and you might want to sit on the steps of the library I love most, at Grand Army Plaza—to think and watch the world go by.

Beware of the slow, creeping isolation that arises from life online—an existence lived within your own head. Don't live a life that makes it too easy to never leave your home. Don't miss out on all the aromas and tastes that keep us warm and human.

Utilizing everything technology has to offer is a good practice, but living your life online is a flat and compromised reality.

Beware the seductive danger of a binary and pixilated existence.

Chapter 20

Great Expectations: A Chapter for Recruiters

"The only power any government has is the power to crack down on criminals. Well, when there aren't enough criminals one *makes* them. One declares so many things to be a crime that it becomes impossible for men to live without breaking laws. Just pass the kind of laws that can neither be observed nor enforced or objectively interpreted—and you create a nation of law-breakers—and then you cash in on guilt. Now that's the system, Mr. Reardon, that's the game, and once you understand it, you'll be much easier to deal with."[15]

—Ayn Rand
Atlas Shrugged (1957)

*N*o book on employment would be complete without a chapter directed to my recruiting buddies and associates across the country.

If you're reading this book and you're still employed as a recruiter, consider yourself lucky. We all know the recruiting industry has been decimated by this oppressive recession. The thin line separating those of us who have a job from those who don't is little more than the grace of God, coupled with a nice run of good luck. I'm hoping you aren't naive enough to think you have this job because you're ten times better than those on the street. If you feel that way, please reconsider. You could be canned tomorrow, with no warning, for a hundred different reasons. The vaporization of American jobs marches on, and none of us know where and when it will stop.

My friend Steve Levy says recruiting is based on connecting people with people. It's imperative to remember that behind each resume is a real person just like you.

You don't have to sympathize endlessly, but a bit of empathy is certainly in order as millions of people struggle to extricate themselves and their families from this new American catastrophe. Let's take a look at how you, as a recruiter, can work with your hiring managers to make life easier for all of us: job hunters, the hiring managers, and yourself. The rub here is that few organizations have a social contract with job seekers. Within the recruiting community there's little agreement about what constitutes a reasonable response to job applicants. I understand that in most cases you can't get back to everyone who engages you. Still, you should follow a few basic rules for interacting with candidates who apply for positions within your company and move through the hiring process.

Once a candidate makes contact with your organization, they have a right to expect fairness and your best effort to do what's right, even if you don't end up hiring them. Let's consider the following as what I see as the most basic of expectations as it relates to your role as a recruiter:

1. *Know What You Want.* For many years I've helped organizations hire new employees. It's astonishing how many companies struggle to develop a position profile that clearly outlines what they want in a new employee. Worse than that are the endless changes they make, usually in the form of additions to the responsibilities and requirements of a profile that's often already unrealistic.

Before you begin interviews for a position, help everyone involved with the hire reach an agreement on what they're looking for in experience and responsibilities. Who should have the last word on the profile? The HM, because the new person is reporting to the HM, who then becomes ultimately responsible for the results of this new employee. Interesting concept? Research Aristotle and his belief in the importance of balancing rights and responsibilities.

When it comes to the interviews, everyone in the interviewing loop should agree with the parameters of the position profile and interview the candidate to that profile only. Anyone not on board with position profile should either remain quiet on this issue or remove themselves from the interviewing team.

> I assure you it's disturbing for a candidate to meet with four different interviewers who have six different ideas about what the real job is all about.

"Let me tell you my version of what this job is really about" is an unsettling and fractured way to begin an interviewing session. This does nothing for the candidate's ability to understand what you need, nor does it speak well for your organization's ability to know where they're going and what they need to get there. The cure? Take an extra few days, a week, or whatever is required to discuss the position in detail so you can reach agreement before you bring in candidates. Then you'll look like the pros we both know you are.

One more thing: get approval on the requisition to hire before you begin interviewing. Going through the torment and time of interviewing, only to be told finance has cut the position just before you're going to make an offer is a tremendous waste of time and resources. It also leaves a lot of people, both inside and outside of the organization, extremely unhappy.

2. Do not discriminate. Your organization doesn't need more people of color. Your organization doesn't need more women, Latinos, Asians, Jews, Martians, or anyone who emigrated here from the planet Neptune. (Okay, maybe a few Neptunians but that's it.) What your organization *does* need is to hire more of the best employees you can identify and attract.

This is all your company will ever need: The best
candidates to support your organizational objectives—
nothing more and nothing less.

T. S. Eliot, the American-born English poet, playwright, and literary critic said, "For us, there is only the trying. The rest is not our business."[16] This thoughtful method of candidate engagement and assessment should guide your every decision.

I am well aware of organizational initiatives to create diversity, reflected in dozens of new rules and requirements that attempt to legislate fairness in hiring. (Fairness can never be legislated, but that's fodder for another book.) If you truly want to be fair and do what's right for your organization and each candidate you interview, then do not discriminate. Ever. Hire on qualifications, always. If you do everything possible to hire the best candidates, you'll create an admirable sense of fairness and equal opportunity for all.

3. Let candidates know where they stand. I had lunch two weeks ago with a friend of mine I'll call Tom, who described his interactions with a company where he interviewed several times. During the process he met with the organization's CEO for two hours. Soon afterward, he went back for a second interview and spent an hour with their CFO. He spoke with them by phone on a third occasion, and they talked about bringing him on board as a consultant. After that, nothing. No return calls from the CEO, the CFO, or anyone else. No response to emails either. Tom considered himself a great fit for this job, which was in his sweet spot—the correct industry and the appropriate size of operation. I know this because I used to work with Tom. There's no excuse for the way this firm handled themselves. Did something change at the company? Did they hire someone's brother-in-law instead? I've never heard Tom say an unkind word about anyone, but this time he was extremely frustrated—and rightfully so. The CEO's reprehensible behavior will be remembered forever. This is not good.

Sadly, this type of a story isn't unusual. I would say the number one gripe of today's candidates is not being told where they stand in the interviewing process. They jump through hoops, hear about the urgency of the position for which they're interviewing, do everything that is requested of them, and provide references to be contacted. And then … nothing. Long, quiet weeks with nary a sound from the very individuals who were frantically searching for a candidate to handle a job called *mission critical*. "Hurry up and wait" is a bad way to do business. It does little to enhance the brand you seek to build and the fans your organization seeks to acquire.

> Failing to communicate with the candidates you hope to recruit and impress makes them absolutely, positively, crazy. I mean big time crazy.

Working inside the organization for so many years made me keenly aware of all the problems associated with actually pulling the trigger and making a hire. The list of things that can and will go wrong is endless. Not only do I understand this, but candidates, on some level, understand it as well. We all know stuff happens. But it must be addressed and communicated. Was the position canceled? Did someone freeze the requisition? Did you hire an internal candidate? Pick up the phone and make the call—now. It's imperative that you, as the person on the inside, do the right thing and tell the candidates in the interviewing loop what's happening. Most of them can handle bad news. Few can handle no news. To remain silent for endless time as candidates simmer is a terrible idea. From a public relations standpoint, this is as bad as it gets.

4. Do not combine two different jobs into one. I do understand we're living in tough economic times. I know we all need to get more bang for the buck with employees we hire. On the other hand, it's silly to create job descriptions that meld two or three jobs into one position. While this may seem like a logical way to save valuable resources, in reality it's most often a very bad idea. First, it greatly reduces the candidate pool of people who fit the position. Secondly, when a new employee begins work with your organization, you should be doing all that you can to increase his chances of success. Combining positions is a sure way to hamper the new employee instead of helping, because trying to merge two roles into one will put him under great pressure. Conflicting priorities, cross-functional demands, and often times contradictory political pressures can lead to serious performance problems. Finally, this type of thinking plays into the "perfect candidate" fantasy employers love to go for in times of high unemployment. There is no perfect candidate, ever. Attempting to find one is a fool's errand. Keep this in mind before you create a Frankenstein position and expect it to be a success.

I've worked inside organizations where people developed position profiles that had endless requirements plus endless responsibilities for the person who was hired. If a person in a meeting said it would be a good idea for the person to do this or that as well, the hiring team would shove the new ideas into the position profile. This is not a good idea, because few people are capable of successfully executing an endless array of different and matrixed and cross-functional responsibilities as they begin a new position. Remember that everything you expect them to handle will take more time than you expect—often a lot more. Beware the out of control position profile; it will generally cause more problems than it solves.

5. Don't wait until the last minute to hire. I was once hired into an organization, and during my first day on the job was summoned to the CEO's office for a briefing. Or so I thought. I was wrong. He wanted me to brief him on my progress. I started work at 9 a.m. that day and the meeting was set for 10 a.m. Even with my poor math skills, I can tell you I was only on the job for one hour. Here is our conversation:

CEO: Where do we stand on new candidates for this, that, and the other account?

Me: I have no idea. This is my first day. I just stated an hour ago.

CEO: You came in here to argue with me? You have no time for that. You're already three weeks behind. Waste time arguing with me, and you will be four weeks behind. You want that?

Me: Uhhh, no—okay.

CEO: Great. Where are we on these candidates?

Do not wait till the last minute to make the hires required to meet your organizational objectives. I urge all recruiters to work closely with hiring managers, not only on the position you're currently looking to fill, but on getting a handle on positions coming down the road for the next quarter.

> Hiring, like surgery, has a higher likelihood for being successful when the process is well thought out, discussed, planned, and properly executed.

No one wants a quadruple bypass, but even worse is having one under emergency conditions at three in the morning in a strange hospital. Waiting until the last moment to hire places a tremendous strain on those involved in the interviewing process: the candidates, and most of all, the new employee. Waiting for the last second to hire and then throwing a new employee into the thick of battle before he knows the ropes or the significant players will reduce his chances for success. Unless it's absolutely unavoidable, do not wait till the last minute to make a hire.

Those who interview candidates know we're in difficult times. You often deal with frightened, frustrated, and angry job seekers. Many of those job candidates were once like you, but in the game of musical chairs, they wound up without a seat at the table. This is a difficult chapter in their lives. They are worried, anxious, and fearful about what lies ahead. You would feel the same way. What do you owe the job seeker? It's hard to say. Go the extra mile? Yes, absolutely. A bit of time, if humanly possible? I think so. I would treat them just as I would want someone to treat my kids, because each and every one of these men and women are in reality, someone's kids.

Give it some thought and be glad you aren't on their side of the table.

6. *A special word to candidates.* If you read this chapter, you must have a sense of how busy recruiters can be and how they struggle with difficult decisions. Think about that before you submit a resume for consideration. Submitting your resume to every job on the planet in hopes that someone will fall in love with your brilliant abilities and hire you, even though you don't fit their needs, is a fantasy. I don't ever remember seeing this happen. Not once. All this activity does is bury the already overburdened recruiter in even more resumes to peruse.

Please, if you do not have at least 70 percent of what's required to meet a position's requirements, do not apply for the job.

Don't waste everyone's time in a futile attempt to make something happen.

Chapter 21
What To Do Now

*"We would like to live as we once lived
but history will not permit it."*
—John F Kennedy

I sit here on Christmas day, editing this manuscript. News of the failing economy, foreclosures, and lives damaged seems endless. It appears the perfect storm has hit us hard. In an article titled "What Happens When the Jobless Give Up," Nina Easton of CNN writes: "The pre-holiday bickering over tax cuts and extending unemployment benefits is drowning out a December government number so frightening it should concentrate the minds of every posturing political leader in Washington: 9.8 percent unemployment. That is staggering; up from when the recession ended 18 months ago, and comes despite signs of recovery in retail, real estate, and corporate profits."[17]

She goes on to quote Narayana Kocherlakota, president of the Federal Reserve Bank of Minneapolis who said in a recent speech, "If history is any guide, this year-plus unemployment rate will only revert to pre-recession levels after several years."

Do I have all the answers? No, and if you're expecting that from me, you have the wrong book. However, I do have a host of ideas that will make a genuine and long term difference for your future. These concepts are reasonable to implement and actionable almost immediately. As I see it, one of the best things one person can offer another is the ability to have a better professional life and a more enriching future. These suggestions offer exactly that opportunity.

Clearly, the time for all of us to make deep and sweeping changes is now: changes in what we do, what we've become, and even to the way we view our world. This is no longer an option—it's a requirement.

Will they tip the scales in your favor by even 30 percent? Probably not, but the big win isn't what you should be looking to achieve. Your goal should be just to get on base, not to hit a home run. Big wins are great, but they most often come to us as the sum of smaller achievements. To gain a 3 percent advantage on one idea, 2 percent on another, and 4 percent on another is the real win. Adding the percentages in a way that tips the scales is what you want to achieve, because the professional goal to which you aspire is at the end of a long line of smaller events. My hope is that you will effectively manage and successfully complete all of these events.

If you swing for the home run every time at bat, you'll miss the ball more often than you hit it. Just pick up a single here and a double there. Just get through the phone screen and do well— that's an accomplishment, an important step. Then get an interview. Fantastic! Then get short-listed and in line for the second interview. Now move forward to the reference phase. All of these are wins by themselves, and it's critical for you to see that. This process isn't just about getting the job—it's about doing well on every step along the way. Those steps, intelligently articulated and played out, are the road map to the end result: the big win we all want to achieve, which is the attainment of our desired professional goal.

What all of us need is an ongoing, focused effort: aggressive intent, combined with the ability to think differently in order to make things happen. We need to work at it long and hard to maximize results. That means being creative and working the angles in ways that are both inspired and innovative so we move closer to our goals. That is my vision for you and for me: a new job, a better job, a career change, a life free of fear and worry—the happy, civilized existence all of us seek to attain. That's what this book is about. That is the home run for which we strive, and I believe it will happen to most of us if we just keep pushing. But there's more.

> How do you feel about this "new normal?" Personally, I struggle with it, and I suspect you do as well. Now we must endure, adjust our thinking, and change with the times.

Like me, you probably had it good not so long ago: nice job, maybe a college education, and great professional experience. Why should you have to endure this for reasons beyond your control? Why should life suddenly become frightful and hard? Why is it necessary for people to suffer over what used to be, in retrospect, so simple and easy? So many people, on some level, just want their father's life: get up, go to work, come home, and do the same thing for a long number of years.

I see future employment, read about it, and think about it every day. I can tell you one thing for certain: the work you and I do in securing employment will reveal strengths and abilities we didn't know we possessed. This strife will make us smarter, faster, and more resourceful. We will develop the capability to envision better solutions and deliver more inspired results because we simply must do that to survive. Perhaps in this unhappy, depressed employment situation we will find our best opportunity to reinvent ourselves— to shine, excel, and persevere in ways we never imagined.

Let's consider twelve things that will transform our lives and inspire change and growth in the lives of those around us.

Read

Did you go to college? Beyond college? Doctorate perhaps? All good things, but not enough. Did you read any of Malcolm Caldwell's work? Surely you've read *Outliers*,[18] if not the rest? How about *The Seven Habits of Highly Effective People*[19] by Covey? What if these book titles come up during an interview? What will you say? "I had no time? I was too busy watching television." We all know studies show reading can improve our lives in many ways, from a higher income level to a longer, more satisfying lifespan. Honestly, can you see the value in reading?

Let me tell you a story. Twenty plus years ago I interviewed for a full time job with a Fortune 500 Company. The interview went well, and I felt great personal chemistry with the interviewer. As we came to a close, he sat quietly for a moment. He folded his hands behind his head, did a small half spin in the chair, and said to me "Tell me, what books have you read lately?" I was stunned. The question came from nowhere and caught me flat footed. I've always been a reader. If you put a book in front of me, I read it. But in the heat of the moment I couldn't remember the titles of the recent books I'd completed. For whatever reason I didn't get that job, but that was okay because my life went in another direction. Did I lose the job because I fell down on that afterthought question? I suspect not, but it was an interesting experience. You might never be asked this question, but then again, you just may. Will you be judged on the books you claim to have read? Probably not, but you'll certainly be judged by the mind you possess that's shaped by those books. Thirty minutes every night is all it takes. You'll never be sorry you read. A lifetime of learning will have value not only in the workplace, but on all the roads you'll travel.

Toastmasters

You've probably heard of Toastmasters—the international organization that helps people master public speaking and gain leadership skills. I can tell you firsthand that it's a great organization. Toastmasters will not only help you improve your speaking abilities, but you'll surround yourself with people who are trying to reach the same goal: better communication, greater confidence, and enhanced professional standing. Since 1924, Toastmasters International has enabled people of all backgrounds to become more confident in front of an audience.

Toastmasters does all it promises—and more. Almost overnight, I've seen quiet, mousy men and women blossom into effective public speakers. In a world that gravitates toward leadership and a bit of flair, the ability to speak before a group is no longer an option. It's a must. Think of someone you admire who achieved prominence and acclaim. I bet that person can speak before groups. Even in high school and college, students need the ability to make presentations. Toastmasters will help you find your own voice, control fear, and develop confidence. The skills you learn through this program will last a lifetime.

Harvey MacKay, author, speaker extraordinaire, and celebrated company president is such a strong believer in Toastmasters that in one of his books he advises readers to join the group for six months. After that time, if the new member doesn't believe he received benefits, MacKay promised to personally refund the membership fee. I joined right after reading that promise and stayed with Toastmasters for five years.

> Someday soon, you may need to articulate your ideas and vision, with high stakes riding on your delivery and ability to communicate. Are you prepared for that moment? I am, and so is Harvey MacKay. You need to be ready as well.

The opportunity to learn and perfect your communication skills in a safe, fun, and highly social environment where people are almost standing in line to help you is a world-class experience. Your big chance to get what you want in life may someday boil down to your ability to present a plan or speak with passion and clarity on your vision, while being sincere and expressing yourself with conviction.

Please join Toastmasters!

No One Needs a Job

I used to be a motorcycle guy. I liked to hang out at a motorcycle guy place that served coffee and fancy little cakes to over-the-hill bikers who rode Ducati and R1150s. One of the guys who held court over there was an electrical engineer on staff at Harvard who did occasional lecturing on a host of topics. He impressed me with his brilliant way of seeing the world. I joined a crowd of five or six guys on a warm Sunday afternoon, where he was deep in conversation with two others. I sat quietly as they discussed employment. That's a topic near and dear to my heart, and I know a thing or two about it. I smirked my best smirk and listened to him wax eloquent. Then it happened. His tangential response to a comment from one of the handful of attendees caught me by surprise. I heard it and looked at him with amazement. Did he say what I just thought he said? I locked eyes with him and blurted, "Could you say that again?"

"I said no one needs a job. No one."

I shot him a second look that could have sunk the Bismarck.

"No one needs a job?" I asked.

"Correct. All people really need is an income."

The world stopped its orbit as a great and elemental truth dropped in front of me. I remember this conversation fondly and have never viewed *job* and *income* in quite the same way since that moment. I hope you can separate these terms in your mind as I have in mine, because they are two profoundly different things.

If you examine this concept closely, you'll see that income is what we need. Income pays the bills and picks up the tab at lunch. Income is required to get those shoes and buy a car. If you had

$10 million in cash buried in the backyard, would you need a job? I wouldn't. You might need work to give your life meaning. You might need work to fill the hours, because after you've had your morning coffee and visited the gym, life can get a bit dull sitting around the house with nothing to occupy your mind or your time. But would you *need* a job with 10 mill in the backyard? I think not.

The problem arises for those of us who don't have big money in the backyard, or a job. Now what? As the saying goes, this is where the real work begins—the work of developing an income. The good news is, many people have discovered their own answers and done quite well. The stories out there of people who've developed creative ways to generate income are astonishing. The number grows every day as the generation of private sector jobs still lies dormant.

For example, I became a consultant and at times a contract worker because I wanted multiple streams of income. I was careful not to place all my eggs in one basket; this time I wanted more control over my destiny. Before that, I worked for a search firm, but it was just one source of revenue to me. And I wanted more. So off I went, to develop new revenue streams. The task wasn't easy, but at least it was my own plan and my own road. I wrote a book and received money for it. I did public speaking and training. More checks. Is this a perfect way to live? No, but I'm able to pay the bills.

How can you do it? As I said in the introduction, this is a book of ideas and concepts. It's about pointing the way and exploring alternatives—forging a new path for yourself and illuminating the possibilities. Definitive answers to semi-impossible questions are not included in this book, but let's give it a shot.

How about selling on eBay? Some people make a killing, while others are just bringing in steady cash. Consulting? You don't need to be the smartest person on the planet, just driven, ready to listen and learn, and able to market your skills and solve some of your client's problems. You don't have to know everything in the world to do this—just more than your client knows. Is that for you?

My friend's son supplements his teaching by charging $80 per hour to tutor. Can you see the possibilities of creative thinking?

What about purchasing a franchise? Studies show franchises are almost seven times more successful than starting the same type of business without franchise support.

How about accepting ground-level work in a new field to see if it interests you? I know a laid-off corporate manager who was so desperate for work he took a job in a local franchise sandwich shop. Turns out, he loved the job—the daily interaction with customers, the camaraderie with his boss and co-workers, and the ability to go home after eight hours without worrying about corporate politics. After a year, the boss opened a second store and promoted the employee to manager. Are there other things you can do in the world of work? Of course. Think about what fits your needs, talents, and lifestyle and don't be afraid to try something new.

Stability? Not!

I remember the words of a Carly Simon song from 1976, from the cut *It Was So Easy Then*.

> "It was so easy then,
> never making any plans
> it was so easy then
> holding hands."

She was right. Life *was* easy back then in so many ways. The big three carmakers owned this country and life was good. My first days in Boston were shaping up well, and I was young. The Data Generals—Wangs, Digitals, and Primes of what was dubbed the "Massachusetts Miracle"—were either in their infancy or beginning to find their groove. Promises of great things were implicit, and I felt invincible. Tracy Kider was a few years away from publishing *Soul of a New Machine* but that machine was on track, and things in the Bay State were rocking. Want a job? Just get a few interviews and you'd score an offer or two. Don't like that job? Get another. No terrorists, no strip searches at the airport, and gas averaged 32 cents a gallon in 1972. Adjusted for inflation, that's about $1.36 today.

Sadly, things change. Those secure times have given way to the new normal under which we must all live. The central question is: How can we live rewarding, civilized lives without a sense of stability? How do we find peace and a sense of calm in a world with no real permanence?

Stability is defined as continuance without change—permanence. To me, as I do the research to define the term, that concept seems almost unreal. Even the Twin Towers, the most permanent things I can imagine, were gone in a flash. After that, nothing can surprise me anymore. *Stability* is just a concept, like *too big to fail*. It was comforting when we had it, but gone now—and it won't be part of our lives anytime soon. A few statistics bring this into focus:

> According to a recent article in the Wall Street Journal, we still have 14.6 million unemployed people looking for work. That's a staggering number; almost too large to understand.

The Labor Department reported a net loss of 131,000 jobs in July, 2010. Want more? In an interview aired by 60 Minutes on December 5, 2010, Federal Reserve Chairman Ben Bernanke—the country's top economist, on the heels of a disappointing jobs report—told 60 Minutes the outlook isn't much brighter. His exact words? "At the rate we're going, it could be four, five years before we are back to a more normal unemployment rate."

Folks, this is very bad news. This 60 Minutes broadcast comes just a couple of days after the government released a jobs report bringing two downbeat surprises: the economy added only 39,000 jobs in November, and the unemployment rate rose to 9.8 percent. We seem to be either standing still or going backward, and that does little to foster stability in our job market.

Am I waxing philosophical? No, not really. I write this because we all need to understand that stability is no longer a fact of life we can count on. I'm sure you remember how it felt to get a regular paycheck. We received benefits, holidays, and a week or two of vacation time. We could get away for awhile, knowing a job awaited us when we returned. We had no Facebook friends; we had *traditional* friends at work, based on familiarity and stability.

I remember it all. I remember the birthday cakes, the occasional lunches out, and the knowledge that we would all be back tomorrow. Things are different now.

Many of us no longer have coworkers—we have clients. We do projects. We look for more projects. We move around and we move on.

Yes, we do live in interesting times, because the only stability we have is the stability we make for ourselves.

Be Like Conan

Many of us watched a real life drama unfold on television when Jay Leno left the Tonight Show, and it was handed off to Conan O'Brian. In the world of professional comedy, it didn't get any bigger than this.

Then all hell broke loose as NBC demonstrated it could do nothing right. The network watched Leno's ratings slip, pulled him back into the 11:30 time slot, and took the Tonight Show away from Conan. The long, clownish scene was painful to watch.

Leno bashed NBC. O'Brian bashed NBC. Every fan of the Tonight Show, a shrine to many fans, bashed NBC. Leno went back and O'Brian was jettisoned, with a ton of cash and a dream cut short. The spectacle played out in the media for weeks. During the last night of his short tenure as the host of the Tonight Show, Conan O'Brian made a personal statement. Here is part of that statement: "All I ask is one thing, and I'm asking this particularly of young people that watch. Please do not be cynical. I hate cynicism. For the record, it's my least favorite quality. It doesn't lead anywhere. Nobody in life gets exactly what they thought they were going to get. But if you work really hard, and you're kind, amazing things will happen. I'm telling you, amazing things will happen."

When I heard this simple statement, I knew it was time for me to change my attitude. I'm not proud of it, but I am probably the most cynical person on the planet. For me, the cup is always half empty, and often it appears to be leaking from the bottom as well. But Conan's words and attitude struck a deep chord within me, and I knew it was time to change. Not tomorrow or next week, but at that exact moment. I recommend you do the same.

Will not being cynical get you a job? Probably not, but does whining and complaining about life's vicissitudes help you any more than it helped me? Then why not give the cynicism a rest? Why not try to find the good in life and think about all the fine things that might come to pass?

Our society tends to view success based upon what we do, not who we are. We love "how to" books that show us how to sell more, get that next big job, or knock their socks off in the interview. This is achievement based upon technique and performance, rather than character. No problem here, but this isn't the entire answer. We need more.

We need not just to *do*, but to *be*. To evolve into a higher level of thinking and living—to become better people instead of people who always know what to say.

We need to pray for more strength as opposed to praying for easier days. Let me assure you, I'm not proselytizing. I come from Brooklyn, NY, and I'm as nuts and bolts as they get, but losing the jaded viewpoint on life is a fine place to begin. I no longer see the value of going through life with a cynical and weary attitude. If it's true that our future depends upon how we perceive the present, then we'll get exactly what we expect from life. Can you see how an attitude change might be long overdue?

"Easy for him to say!" Is that what you're mumbling? Trust me, this is not any easier for me than it is for you. You went on an interview last week and someone else got the job? You knew things were rigged against you from the beginning, right? No way you'd get that job. And you were right. Did that jaded thinking do anything positive for you? Did it make you feel good? Was it an uplifting experience to exist in a place with no possibilities or hope? I believe not, and that is exactly why we need to lose the cynical attitude. So much of life is a choice. I choose to leave my long standing negative attitude behind. I want a better existence for me and for you. I hope you will follow me and take this to heart.

Cold Calling Is Good

Bill Russell, a famous Boston Celtic of times gone by, once said, "Hustle is talent." He was right, of course. Hustle is one of the things that often means the difference between success and almost success. And that's where the fine art of cold calling comes into play.

Nothing strikes more fear into the hearts of most people then cold calling. This is the *sit at your desk* version of public speaking, and some of the smartest, most articulate folks I know are terrified by the mere thought of making a cold call. All this fuss is quite unnecessary, and the fear of this bogyman is unwarranted. Cold calling can yield big results for very little effort—and that type of return comes in handy when you need results fast.

The first time I practiced cold calling with a trainer, she went into the other room to role play with me. I needed to say only a few words, and she would handle the rest. She told me it was like softball—simple and easy.

My heart was pounding. I dialed her on the intercom and she said hello. I opened my mouth to speak—and instantly froze. I tried to speak and no words came out. This was a humbling experience, but I pushed through it and everything fell into place, because that's what cold calling is all about.

Cold calling is a lost art on some levels. That's a sad thought, because there are times nothing else will do; nothing else will bring the desired result.

> I can tell you some of the best work I've ever done, the finest results I've ever obtained, and the best relationships, came from cold calling.

It is direct and aggressive in a good way, and one of the best door openers for opportunity. I guarantee cold calling can work well for you if you consider it to be a tool for progress, and use that tool when you see it's appropriate.

When I began working as a recruiter after leaving the agency business, I used to call Bill once a week or so to touch base. Bill was a VP of Human Resources at an excellent company. I liked him and sensed an opportunity, because he could teach me a lot. Quite honestly, I needed a mentor and Bill was the guy. I remember calling him one day, and after we chatted a bit, he got quiet. Then we had the following conversation.

"I just had a frightening thought. You're never going to stop calling me are you?" said Bill.

"No," I said. "The kids need shoes, and I can really help you with recruiting."

"Okay. Get your ass in here on Monday," he said. "We'll have lunch and see if we can't find you something to do here, because I can't live this way with you calling all the time."

I was in!

That came from a cold call. I was hired to recruit for three months as a result of Bill's edict, and I recruited there for almost four years. My biggest clients were all cold calls. Every single one.

No e-mails for the junk folder, no fancy brochures, no press kit. All cold calls, which was, and still is, a great way to make things happen, because you have the person you wish to speak with right there on the phone. You have the ability to tell that person what you want and how it will benefit them. It's clear, in the moment, and a daring sweep of confidence, power, and control.

What makes us all so fearful? What is it about cold calling that makes us swallow hard and pray the person is out and we get voice mail? The fear of rejection. That's the big killer. The fear of the other person saying he doesn't want to talk to you—that you're bothering him. How dare you call, just say hello, and start talking. In short; who the hell do you think you are?

With that in mind, let's address this fear. Rejection is part of life. Friends, lovers, and many other people will reject us during our lives. We, in turn, will do the same to others. It's all part of the game of life. Being rejected during a cold call because someone doesn't know you is why we use the term cold call. If you had an introduction, a person whose name to use as a recommendation, then it would be a warm call and might seem easier. Someone rejects you; so what? Even if the person tells you he has no time, stop bothering him, and hangs up on you, it's no big deal. The rejection doesn't matter, because you're just a voice on the phone to them, nothing more.

If you're working on a list to make a number of cold calls, just smile and move on to the next. Tomorrow, if required, you will make cold calls again. You'll do a great job, try to make progress with those who talk with you, and forget about the ones who hung up on you. It's their loss. Sooner or later, a cold call will lead to a conversation or an appointment for a conversation, an interview, or whatever you're hoping to find. I suggest you forget the ones who reject you and remember those ones who become friends or customers.

I must admit to a real weakness, and I suggest that if cold calling is part of your game plan, you develop this weakness as well. When

I make a cold call, I honestly can't imagine a single person out there who won't be interested in what I have to say. Not even one. I call because I represent opportunity; I represent a bridge to the next step in a career or as the solution to a client's most difficult hiring issues. My call is a good news call. You must see your call as a good news call as well. Make the call professional. Speak no longer than required. Be polite and to the point. Be friendly. Be a good listener. Thank the person for making time to speak with you by phone.

What's the best reason to cold call? Because you have the name and number of someone you might influence *on whatever it is you're seeking* in a way that will benefit you and them. It's much easier than you think. Cold calling is a world class skill with a human and interpersonal touch. If you can get your arms around it, you'll be glad you did.

Value Is King

This flies in the face of the belief that the customer is king, but in reality, the customer is only king if you provide value. If you fail to offer anything of value, why would anyone be your customer? Can you see how Honda and Toyota massacred the big three auto makers and beat them at the game of selling cars? A game, I am chagrined to point out, that we in America invented? Can you see how they even went so far as to develop luxury divisions such as Lexus, and went on to kill us there as well? It's all about value, and value must be at top of mind as you move forward in your search for a new position. You must represent yourself as a providential holder of great value for the organization with which you're interviewing. This isn't always an easy thing to do, because people often cannot see the value they bring to the table. Let me give you a definitive example of my value to a client.

About a dozen years ago, I was searching for a financial person who could restructure a small chemical company and handle general administrative duties for the company's president and founder. I charged a flat fee of $15,000 for that search and the compensation level for the position was in the $75,000 range. I located three or four candidates, and they selected one after the interviews were completed. I closed the deal and the candidate started work after giving two weeks' notice to his former employer. At the time, the new employer was barely doing $1 million per year in sales or revenue, and was losing money. Years later, as of my last call I placed to the candidate, the company is doing $26 million annually, thanks to this candidate's strong ability to dovetail with sales and develop strategic revenue partnerships on an international scale. Do you see the value I brought to that client? My fee was easily worth ten times what I charged. That is value on a grand scale.

Tell me, do you ever think of your value? If not, you should, because if you don't recognize it, how will anyone else know?

When you prepare for an interview, be ready to tell the interviewer, in no uncertain terms, about your value. Did you bring in your last project under budget and save the company 9 percent of a two million dollar budget? Say it loud. Use that exact word: VALUE.

You need to make your value absolutely clear. "I brought a lot of value to my last position. I saved $100,000 as a result of my project and did the job of an employee who left because they never replaced him." Good HMs search for advantage and enhanced effectiveness when interviewing. They look for value and for a reason to make a hire. If you assume they'll connect the dots on their own and *discover* the value, you sell yourself short. Point out the value, and you will be doing your job in the interview. Represent yourself in terms of the value you've brought to other organizations, and speak honestly of your accomplishments. If you can manage to do this, you'll have a clear advantage over the competition

Embrace the New Face of Work

The emerging new workplace will offer amazing opportunities, but also requires different abilities and an adjusted mindset.

For starters, the era of getting paid for just showing up is over. The days of calling your administrative assistant and telling her to turn on your computer and hang your jacket on the back of your chair so people think you're in the office are a thing of the past. For the sake of your company, and for your sake as well, you need to represent ongoing value or you need to be gone. Just as a ticket stub is your proof of admission to the big game, value and ongoing contribution are your tickets to continued employment.

> The days of living today on what you did last year are history. "What have you done for me lately?" is the new maxim.

Looking for continued employability? Make continued contributions of real value, and you'll likely get what you want. Fail to do so and things may end badly. Want a sense of stability in employment? Create it by demonstrating real and measurable value.

Start To Like Everyone

Not crazy about minorities? Get over it. This is America, and unless you're Native American, one of your ancestors came over in a boat and signed the registry at Ellis Island, as did mine.

We need to play nicely with others, because warring in the workplace will come to no good for either the winners or the losers. The old saying "Only a fool fights in a burning house" has never made more sense.

> The days of everyone looking a lot like you in the workplace are over. We are multicultural, multiethnic, and multiracial. Truth be told, we are multi everything.

Have a problem with Geeks? I suggest you change your thinking. Someone once said, "Be nice to them, because someday you'll probably work for one." Like your computer and your smart phone? Enjoying the 56-inch flat screen with surround sound? Thank a geek, because if not for them you'd be sitting around a campfire singing songs instead of using that Blackberry.

How about women? Does seeing them in management and leadership positions bother you? If so, you're in huge trouble, because women are going to work in America and they mean business. "Women are knocking on the door of leadership at the very moment when their talents are especially well matched with the requirements of the day," writes David Gergen in the introduction to *Enlightened Power: How Women Are Transforming the Practice of Leadership.*[20]

The future will be rosy for those who contribute; those who can get along, build consensus, collaborate, think independently, and solve problems. Women in the workplace are not only here to stay—they're here to do, create, and build great things. The authors of an article in *Time Magazine* dated May 14, 2009 entitled "Women Will Rule Business"[22] said of women: "They're consensus builders, conciliators, and collaborators, and they employ what is called a transformational leadership style—heavily engaged, motivational, extremely well suited for the emerging, less hierarchical workplace." Translation? They will be far more suited for the less top down and testosterone-oriented, male-dominated industries we will soon see emerging. Do you come from a country where oppressing women is part of your culture? I see two choices for you. Change your attitude or change you address, because women are here to stay.

Embrace Technology and Go to Work

At one time, going to work meant getting on public transportation or driving your car to work. This is still the case in many positions, but other possibilities have opened as technology and emerging marketplaces create new ways to contribute, collaborate, and add the value required to generate income.

The original concept of *going to work* is tied to the industrial revolution, when people moved away from the agricultural model and began working together in a physical location. In this model, which we still follow today to a certain extent, everyone is employed by the same organization in a hierarchical structure. Such organizations have little flexibility.

Workers sit at a station, and a manager occasionally looks in to see if everyone is busy. Because of the nature of the tasks, it isn't feasible to work away from the site; workers need machines and tools only available at the company.

And so the concept of *butts in chairs* came to exist. I find it interesting how so many managers, even today, seem to find comfort in the fact that the people who work for them are seated in the office. They don't necessarily look at metrics to measure performance, they check to see if you're present. I mention this to demonstrate a bit of folly in an outdated business model.

Of course, some jobs will always require a physical presence. The woman who drives a train must be there. The cook and the waiter must be present. The emergency room doctor must be there. But what about the editor, the software engineer, the researcher, the recruiter, and the social networking consultant? Do those people need to spend time, money, and gas driving to a company office when they could be more productive at home? I suspect not. Aside from the occasional bit of face time for a meeting or an occasional lunch to build relationships, one can do great things and seldom leave the home office.

I believe we are on the cusp of seeing a new and emerging workplace—a place with fewer cubicles and more flexibility. A workplace that is technology heavy, where those who embrace new technology will be rewarded. I, for one, am happy to see a bit more of this enlightened and flexible state of mind. I believe the nature of work has changed, and will continue to evolve as technology helps us become more efficient.

My advice for your future is to embrace technology and use it. Keep up with the curve. If something's new, take the challenge, even if it doesn't seem like part of your world.

If emerging technology is a part of your world at work, know it backwards and forward. Are you annoyed by the fact that the minute you figure out one technology, something new comes along? Me too, but that's the nature of technology. Go with the flow, embrace the new, and try to have fun. Falling behind isn't a good thing for your business, your career, or your life.

Back Off on the Stuff

Forgive me if I'm not impressed by your $5,000 Rolex. Sad to say, that watch doesn't make you look more sophisticated or like the skipper of a big racing yacht. It doesn't lead me to think you have European lineage or you're a master of the boardroom. What it does make me think is that somehow the advertising machine on Madison Avenue convinced you it's better to shell out five grand to know the time than to own a Swiss Army watch for a fraction of the cost.

Every penny we spend represents money we had to go out and earn. In these times, earning money isn't all that easy. For some of us, it's almost impossible. We need to make a seismic shift in how we all spend money—and the good news is, that change isn't as difficult as you might think. All we need to do is reduce the amount of money we spend for unnecessary things. With the economy melting down before our eyes, many of us are in a financial jail we built for ourselves one bar at a time. This is not a good thing.

Understand me. I'm not preaching, and I don't want to take away anyone's fun, mine included. On the other hand, we all have so much stuff that it fills every corner of our homes and garages. Many people actually have to purchase storage space in large climate-controlled facilities to store extra stuff they can't keep at home. How strange is that?

Can you see that everything we have costs us hard-earned money, even in the best of times? I believe we all need to spend more on what we need and less on things we don't need.

As an example, let's take a stroll through my closet.

I own nine suits, 41 shirts, 16 pair of pants, endless tee shirts, too many ties to count and two pair of Lucasi cowboy boots. (I got the first pair after two martinis on an empty stomach in Dallas, but that's a story for a different book.) Do you see my point? Why does a guy from Brooklyn need cowboy boots in the first place, let alone Lucasis? Surely all this stuff is a bit much for a guy who showers in the morning, and unless he's seeing a client, wears the same clothing almost every day. I assure you there is far more stuff in my closet then I mention here. I'm embarrassed to admit I can't figure out what some of that stuff is, or why I bought it in the first place.

I've gone through four motorcycles, including two Honda Valkyries, and more Maxima's then I can count. I won't even begin to discuss my fountain pen fetish. Sound systems? An endless number. All that money is gone. I don't need all of that stuff, and in a heartbeat I'd return it for the money I wasted to get it. I'm willing to bet many of you own even more stuff than I have. I believe it's time to cut back. This doesn't mean you'll be doomed to a diminished, less enriching life. It means your purchases should to be better thought out and less impulse oriented. Do you truly believe you're sexier in a $1,400 blazer? I think not.

Have you spent $75 for ties and bought $200 shirts? Are you driving a five series? Did know that the new GTI with a gearbox smokes and handles like it's on rails for half the price? Give it some thought. Spending money to impress others is costly, usually doesn't work, and leaves you with a big tab. As times change, you may realize the best way to impress others is to take the path of the minimalist by impressing them with your brains and good judgment.

Someone once said, "He who owns many things is owned by many things." I believe this is true.

Rethink Retirement

A Google search on the word *retirement* brings up 83,200,000 hits. Obviously, lots of people are thinking about, advising about, and writing about retirement. This might be a good thing, but I have doubts regarding the traditional picture of retirement we Americans hold so dear. I mean the retirement where you get a gold watch, a nice dinner, and the rest of your time on this planet is yours to do with as you please. Sleep till noon? Go to Vegas? Get an RV and cruise the country? Anything you like. That all sounds good, and if it's what you want, then I hope you get it. On the other hand, I have grave concerns that the American dream of retirement was appropriate for a time gone by, but isn't realistic today. Before long, we may be looking at a new type of retirement, instead of transitioning into a life of strange hats, early bird specials, and polyester shorts.

According to the World Bank, life expectancy in the United States (averaging the ages of men and women) is almost 79 years. That number is expected to rise with the availability of advanced health care and other lifestyle enhancements. This is a big change from the lifespan of only 69.2 years (averaged for men and women) back in 1960, based upon Social Security actuarial tables. As we live longer and more of us retire, there won't be enough money to support retirement as an institution in this country. Furthermore, we're dealing with retirement of the largest generation in the history of this country—the Baby Boomers.

Seventy-eight million baby boomers born between 1946 and 1964 are reaching retirement age at a rapid clip. At some point, our economy won't be able to support all those who wish to retire. Furthermore, few can afford to live on Social Security, and with the immense losses realized in privately subsidized retirements when the economy crashed, many people will be working far longer than they ever hoped to stay employed. Strangely enough, this might not be as bad as we expect.

Most of the retired people I know don't seem all that happy. I'm not a sociologist and have no data, but I'm not impressed with retirement—especially since the next major life event is often death. I intend to put that off for a bit. Is it possible working longer isn't such a negative thing?

> Rather than be disappointed with a modified retirement, it might be a good idea to reassess what retirement can mean for you. Perhaps now is the time to have a personal financial planner help you to map out the kind of retirement you seek.

To develop a new and more realistic outlook on retirement, think about what it will be like and when retirement happens for you. Perhaps the new retirement model will have room for many things you hope to do, while you're still earning enough income to fund your lifestyle. The "perhaps" factors of retirement in the years to come are endless, but speculation isn't the mission of this manuscript. I just hope we all have what it takes to see this is a different America than in years gone by. We need to adjust to economic realities and adapt with new sets of eyes that see different options. Furthermore, we need to do it in a way that allows us to live our days with the rewards we worked so hard to achieve.

So there we have it: 12 things to consider. Are there more things we can be and more we can do? I suspect so. I don't have all the answers, and I question those who say they do. On the other hand, I believe this is good place to start. It's a good place to sit down and understand the world has changed, and what has worked in the past needs careful consideration. Will all things stated above work for everyone? No, again, but I believe there's something here for everyone to consider, apply, and use to great advantage; something to tip the scales enough on any given day so you just might hit that home run; something to restore a bit of satisfaction and optimism to all aspects of our lives.

Chapter 22
Closing Thoughts

"We shall neither fail nor falter; we shall not weaken or tire ...
give us the tools and we will finish the job."
—Winston Churchill

*W*e are finally here—at the end pages of this book, but not
the end of the road. This is a good place to consider the
possibilities and open our minds to wonderful things that lie ahead.

I've looked forward to writing this part of the book since my
first keystrokes. I knew it would be fun. I want you to know I wrote
his entire book in 23 days. Not an easy thing to do—and if you
write, you can appreciate that. Why the manic ride? Because one
day I sat up ramrod straight in my chair and realized this book
had to be written. It had to be written by me, and it had to be
written immediately. I feel this way because I see the need for this
information to get out there. Now that the writing is over, in some
ways I miss it. Perhaps that's what happens when the dream is over:
an odd sense of emptiness and aloneness follows.

Whether you're looking for another job, a better job, or simply
struggling to achieve greater professional goals, I believe what I've
written here will give you a new vantage point.

I hope you'll consider all I've suggested and discussed in the previous pages. If I said anything with which you disagree, I can only say this:

It isn't my intention to win you over. It is my intention for you to win.

Thoughts or comments?

Please email me at howard@employmentrage.com

Further and ongoing info?

My blog: http://www.employmentrage.com

Twitter: @howardadamsky

End Notes

1. Barbara Ehrenreich, *Bait and Switch The (Futile) Pursuit of the American Dream* (Metropolitan Books; 1st edition, September 8, 2005).

2. Robert Townsend, *Up the Organization* (Fawcett, December 12, 1981).

3. Dominique Browning, *Slow Love: How I Lost My Job, Put on My Pajamas and Found Happiness* (Atlas (May 9, 2010).

4. Harvey MacKay, *Swim With the Sharks Without Getting Eaten Alive, Outsell, Outmanage, Outmotivate, and Outnegotiate Your Competition* (Ballantine Books, August 27, 1996).

5. Victoria Strauss, "When Asking for Help," Writer Beware Blogs, May 24, 2010. http://accrispin.blogspot.com/2010/05/when-asking-for-help.html

6. "Forty-five Percent of Employers Use Social Networking Sites to Research Job Candidates, CareerBuilder Survey Finds," Chicago, August 19, 2009. Jennifer Grasz, www.careerbuilder.com

7. Thomas Friedman, *The World is Flat* (Picador July 24, 2007).

8. Kaplan, Andreas M.; Michael Haenlein (2010). "Users of the world, unite! The challenges and opportunities of Social Media". Business Horizons 53 (1): 59–68. doi:10.1016/j.bushor.2009.09.003. ISSN 0007-6813. http://www.sciencedirect.com/science/article/B6W45-4XFF2S01/2/600db1bd6e0c9903c74 4aaf34b0b12e1 Retrieved 2010-09-15.

9. Alvin Toffler, *Future Shock* (Bantam; 1 edition (June 1, 1984), http://www.alvintoffler.net/

10. Robin Dunbar, *How Many Friends Does One Person Need?: Dunbars Number and Other Evolutionary Quirks* (Harvard University Press (November 1, 2010).

11. Dan Schawbel *Me 2.0: Build a Powerful Brand to Achieve Career Success* (Kaplan Publishing; Original edition, March 31, 2009).

12. Curtis Silver, "Fighting the Fear of Social Media," (http://www.wired.com/geekdad/2009/09/social-media-fighting-the-fear/).

13. Brian Solis, Deirdre Breakenridge, *Putting the Public Back in Public Relations: How Social Media Is Reinventing the Aging Business of PR* (FT Press; 1 edition, March 1, 2009). You Tube video: http://www.youtube.com/watch?v=BbolypsRfXg

14. Chris Brogan, www.chrisbrogan.com.

15. Ayn Rand, *Atlas Shrugged*, (Plume August 1, 1999).

16. T.S. Eliot, *Four Quartets*, 1945 (Mariner Books March 20, 1968).

17. Nina Easton, "What Happens When the Jobless Give Up," December 13, 2010, http://money.cnn.com/2010/12/10/news/economy/long_term_unemployment.fortune/index.htm

18. Malcom Gladwell, *Outliers: The Story of Success*, (Little, Brown and Company; 1 edition (November 18, 2008).

19. Covey, Steven R., *The Seven Habits of Highly Effective People*, (Free Press; 1st edition September 15, 1990) http://www.amazon.com/s/ref=nb_sb_ss_i_0_43?url=searchalias%3Dstripbooks&field-keywords=the+seven+habits+of+highly+effective+people&sprefix=the+seven+habits+of+highly+effective+people

20. Lin Coughlin (Editor), Ellen Wingard (Editor, Keith Holihan (Editor) *Enlightened Power: How Women Are Transforming the Practice of Leadership* (Jossey-Bass; 1 edition, April 15, 2005).

21. *Time Magazine*, "Women Will Rule Business" May 14, 2009. , http://www.time.com/time/specials/packages/article/0,28804,1898024_ 1898023_1898078,00.html

About the Author

Howard Adamsky has been recruiting since 1985 and is an industry expert on making great hires. As a consultant, writer, and public speaker, he works with organizations to support their efforts in building great companies. He holds a bachelor's degree from the CUNY at Brooklyn College, with graduate work in counseling psychology at Boston State College.

Adamsky authored *Hiring and Retaining Top IT Professionals/The Guide for Savvy Hiring Managers and Job Hunters Alike* published by Osborne/McGraw-Hill as part of the Computerworld Books for IT Leaders series. He regularly consults with senior management teams, coaching them on hiring/closing tactics, interviewing skills, long range staffing plans, performance management, employee retention strategies, employee development programs, and problem/poor performance employee work-outs.

Adamsky is a politically incorrect, atypical thinker who solves problems and gets results. His work has made an enormous difference with his clients as he supercharges the talent acquisition process and hires smart, motivated employees. He is a regular contributor to ERE Media, a Certified Internet Recruiter, and a Certified Diversity Recruiter.

Available from NorlightsPress and fine booksellers everywhere

Toll free: 888-558-4354   **Online:** www.norlightspress.com
Shipping Info: Add $2.95 - first item and $1.00 for each additional item

Name _____

Address _____

Daytime Phone _____

E-mail _____

No. Copies	Title	Price (each)	Total Cost
	Subtotal		
	Shipping		
	Total		

Payment by (circle one):
  Check   Visa   Mastercard   Discover   Am Express

Card number_____3 digit code_____

Exp.date_____ Signature_____

Mailing Address:

2323 S.R. 252
Martinsville, IN 46151

Sign up to receive our catalogue at
www.norlightspress.com

LaVergne, TN USA
22 January 2011
213511LV00001B/25/P